Grammar Teachers' Book 4

Contents

Introduction

"Like everything metaphysical, the harmony between thought and reality is to be found in the grammar of language." *(Ludwig Wittgenstein, philosopher)*

"There is a satisfactory boniness about grammar which the flesh of sheer vocabulary requires before it can become a vertebrate and walk the earth."
(Anthony Burgess, author)

"I believe that every English poet should master the rules of grammar before he attempts to bend or break them." *(Robert Graves, poet)*

Each of these three quotations expresses a different, but equally pertinent argument for the importance of learning grammar.

- Grammar is the means by which a person's ideas are meaningfully communicated. A person's ideas, no matter how good, are of little practical importance unless he or she can express them clearly.
- Words only become imbued with meaning when they are placed within the grammatical structure of carefully crafted sentences.
- The rules of grammar need not be a straitjacket. On the contrary, knowledge of the rules enables confident speakers and writers to adapt them creatively to maximise the effectiveness of their communication for particular purposes and audiences.

Key Grammar is a series of books designed to help children practise essential grammar and punctuation skills needed to progress successfully through primary school. Supporting all UK national curricula, the series provides the reiteration, practice and consolidation that is so necessary to children's learning once the initial explicit, interactive teaching has taken place.

WHAT IS GRAMMAR?

Grammar is the system and structure of a language – the conventions which govern the relationship between words in order to make meaning. Grammar rules and guidelines help both speakers and writers to use language effectively to convey what they mean. Grammar is part of the general study of language called "linguistics".

Punctuation is a toolbox of marks and signs that serve to organise grammatical structures to make the meaning clearer to the reader. Some marks signpost, in written English, the pauses and stops that occur naturally in spoken English. They can indicate not only where a pause should occur, but also how long that pause should be. A comma, for example, indicates a shorter pause than does a full stop. Other marks, such as the question and exclamation marks, convey inflections in the voice. Marks, such as apostrophes and speech marks, provide clarification: apostrophes indicate possession or omission; speech marks indicate direct speech or quotation.

WHY GRAMMAR MATTERS

There are few things one can learn which are as important as the ability to speak and write effectively. Providing children with a detailed understanding of how language works will empower them to use and manipulate it in a variety of exciting ways. It will enable them to explore their ideas more fully orally and to find a "written" voice that expresses exactly what they want to communicate with precision and appeal.

TEACHING AND LEARNING GRAMMAR

The mere whisper of grammar often evokes negative feelings in teachers, associated with either a lack of confidence in the subject themselves, or a memory of dry and boring grammar lessons when they were pupils. However, the process by which children learn how words work and how to craft them into sentences that mean and do exactly what they want them to do can be an intriguing and rewarding adventure.

Building on intuitive knowledge
We all learn our own language naturally. Children come to school already knowing a great deal about the grammar of English. However, much of their understanding is *implicit*. Grammar teaching is about building on children's intuitive knowledge and then making that knowledge *explicit*.

Developing a technical vocabulary
Teaching grammar also involves providing children with a vocabulary set in which to discuss language. Every school subject has its own specific vocabulary, composed of technical terms used to talk about the subject. In maths, for example, it is important for children to know such words as *digit, numerator, factor, integer* and *decimal*; and, in science, such words as *evaporation, friction, conductors, orbit* and *organism*. The study of language is no exception: children need to know the terms of grammar and to be able to use them fluently when talking about their writing. For example, it is much easier to discuss errors of subject–verb agreement if children actually know and understand the terms "subject" and "verb".

Practical pointers
In the teaching of grammatical skills, teachers should seek to:
- Encourage children to show grammatical awareness when reading, explaining, for example, the use of commas, speech marks, exclamation marks and question marks.
- Make links between texts read and the texts children are asked to generate.
- Revisit the skills practised in *Key Grammar* during weekly creative writing sessions.
- Instil as much enthusiasm into the writing process as in the reading process.
- Employ a wide range of writing styles with the children, not limiting their grammatical practice to, for example, narrative writing or report writing.
- Model writing as much as possible, including proofreading.
- Comment on children's work, as appropriate to the child, with regard to specific grammar skills currently being taught/practised.

- Set clear grammar targets for differentiated groups – for example, by using the *Try it out!*, *Keep practising!* and *Take up the challenge!* sections of *Key Grammar* to aid differentiated planning, and the extension activities to extend and follow up focused practice.
- Collect, discuss and classify appropriate words and phrases in classroom displays to reinforce the grammar skills being taught and practised.

KEY GRAMMAR COMPONENTS AND STRUCTURE

Key Grammar comprises five Pupil's Books, five Workbooks and five Teachers' Guides aimed at Years 2–6 (Primary 2/3–7).

Pupil's Books

The Pupil's Books provide self-contained units of work, each of which focuses on a particular concept or rule, the **key idea**. There are three sets of activities in each unit. These offer a simple progression that can be used for differentiation:

- **Try it out!**
  An activity to check the child's understanding of the rule or concept reiterated in the "key idea".
- **Keep practising!**
  An activity for the child to practise, develop and consolidate learning of the "key idea".
- **Take up the challenge!**
  An activity that requires the child to apply their learning in new ways or to extend the learning. Sometimes there is an *Extra challenge* aimed at stretching the more able children.

Assessment units are included to track progress and to enable teachers to diagnose areas of difficulty that may need extra attention. There are three assessment units in each book to allow for termly assessment. Teachers may ask children to complete an entire assessment unit in one go, or they may wish to use individual activities to test children's learning in one key area. Assessment in Key Grammar is intended to be formative, and therefore children's involvement in assessing their own progress is vital. To this end, you may also wish to photocopy relevant answer pages in the Teachers' Guide so that children can mark their own work from the answers provided.

A glossary is included at the back of each Pupil's Book to provide an easy reference tool. It lists and explains grammatical terms and technical vocabulary relevant to the topics addressed in the book. Examples are given where appropriate.

Workbooks

A write-in Workbook accompanies each Pupil's Book and provides additional practice of key grammar skills. The units in the Workbook mirror those in the Pupil's Book and the activities can be used for a variety of purposes – for example:
- immediate consolidation following completion of the Pupil's Book unit;
- subsequent revisiting of a key skill for revision or prior to work on extending that skill;

- differentiated practice for individuals needing support or extension in a particular area;
- homework.

Teachers' Guides

The Teachers' Guides provide brief introductory information on the reasons for teaching grammar and the importance for children of focused and regular practice of key skills. This is followed, in each Guide, by notes, answers and extension activities related to each unit in the Pupil's Book, answers to Workbook activities and photocopiable masters.

Unit-by-unit notes on the Pupil's Book

The bulk of the Teachers' Guides is devoted to unit-by-unit teacher information, answers to the activities, a suggested mark scheme and a range of ideas for extension work. These are presented under the following headings:

- **Focus:** the objective of the unit as reflected in the "key idea" of the Pupil's Book.
- **Teacher information:** useful subject knowledge for teachers and/or strategies, ideas or hints that might make the learning easier/more efficient for the children.
- **Answers to Pupil's Book:** answers to *Try it out!*, *Keep practising!* and *Take up the challenge!* activities in the Pupil's Book. Although many of the answers provided are single words or phrases (for economy of space), it is always valuable for pupils to answer in full sentences in order to develop good practice from the outset. In some places, open-ended questions invite a variety of possible answers and, where this is the case, guidance is given on the kinds of response that are acceptable. The answers also include a suggested mark scheme (see under "Suggested mark scheme" below).
- **Extension activities:** follow-up activity ideas to enable children to explore the "key idea" further and offer opportunities for further work in grammar, other language work and writing.

Suggested mark scheme

To help teachers who wish to record and track children's performance in the activities, a suggested mark scheme is provided. This marks each 2-page unit out of 30 and each 4-page unit out of 60 and allows some flexibility for awarding marks for aspects such as spelling and handwriting as well, should that be deemed appropriate. The suggested mark scheme is also given in the Pupil's Book and Workbook to make children aware of how their performance may be marked, and also to encourage them to be involved in their own target setting.

Answers to Workbook

The answers to the Workbook activities are given, unit by unit, in a separate section. This facilitates the use of the Workbooks as a standalone element.

Photocopiable masters

The final section of each Teachers' Guide contains a selection of photocopiable masters including: activities for revision or extension; investigations; puzzles and games.

HOW TO USE KEY GRAMMAR

Key Grammar is intended for use in small-group, paired and independent grammar and punctuation practice work, following explicit, interactive teaching of the key ideas. The series supports all UK national curricula and follows the objectives of the NLS and its associated programmes such as *Developing Early Writing* and *Grammar for Writing*.

As the key ideas are reiterated and exemplified at the beginning of each unit, children will probably be able to tackle the units with the minimum of teacher intervention. However, it is often helpful if the teacher talks through the unit first and explains exactly what it is that they are being asked to do.

The units are designed to be tackled in the order arranged. Where key ideas are revisited within a book, there is a progression, with a subsequent unit building on the previous one. However, each unit is self-contained to allow flexibility so teachers may choose to take some units out of order if a particular key idea is relevant to current class work or individual needs.

A WORD ABOUT...

Punctuation

There are different schools of thought about *when* punctuation should be inserted in the process of writing. Because punctuation is so closely related to meaning, some writers like to punctuate as they go along. Other writers, however, prefer to concentrate first on getting their ideas onto paper and then to go back over their writing, putting in the necessary punctuation to make their writing clear. This latter method is part of proofreading which, in any case, should be an integral stage in the process of writing. Children should be taught that a piece of writing should never be considered "finished" until it has been proofread properly.

Practice through extended writing

Practice activities, focused on discrete topics, are valuable in developing fluency in grammatical and punctuation usage. However, it is vital that children be encouraged to carry over into their extended writing the rules, guidelines and principles they have learned.

The use of grammar skills in writing should always be clearly presented to the children and enable them to recognise its use within a wide range of genres (stories, lists, information texts and procedural writing). Children should develop a growing awareness of the purpose of the writing they are engaged in and its intended audience. As their skills develop, children should be expected to draft and redraft their work, paying attention to the length, genre and the intended audience.

KEY GRAMMAR BOOK 4 AND THE NATIONAL CURRICULA

Unit	NLS objectives	England: English in the National Curriculum — KS2 POS: En3 Writing; Knowledge, skills and understanding: Composition, Planning and drafting, Punctuation and Standard English	Scotland: English Language 5–14 Guidelines — POS: Writing; Strand: Punctuation and structure, handwriting and presentation and Knowledge about language Levels C–E	Wales: English in the National Curriculum — KS2 POS: Writing; Skills	Northern Ireland: English in the National Curriculum — KS2 POS: Writing; Range: Expected Outcomes
1 Word classes	6.1.S1	Key Grammar provides pupils with activities to: • 1e use features of layout, presentation and organisation • 2 practise note-taking, summarising, drafting, editing and proof-reading • 6a investigate how written standard English varies in degrees of formality • 6b investigate some of the differences between standard and non-standard English usage • 7a understand word classes and the grammatical functions of words, including nouns, verbs, adjectives, adverbs, pronouns, prepositions, conjunctions, articles • 7b understand and identify features of different types of sentences, including statements, questions and commands • 7c understand and practise the grammar of complex sentences, including clauses, phrases and connectives • 7d understand the purposes and features of paragraphs, and how ideas can be linked.	Key Grammar provides pupils with activities to: • understand the terms noun, verb, adjective, adverb, pronoun, conjunction – and identify words appropriately • understand the terms comma, question mark, quotation mark, apostrophe, punctuation – and use them correctly • understand the terms: singular, plural, tense, subject, clause, audience and purpose – and use and identify examples appropriately • structure and punctuate sentences and paragraphs • indicate speech • achieve some variety in sentence structure • link sentences of different lengths and organise them into paragraphs to shape meaning • write in a variety of forms to communicate key events, facts, points of view, using appropriate organisation and specialist vocabulary	Key Grammar provides pupils with activities to: • 2.5 use punctuation marks correctly in their writing • 2.8 use features of layout and presentation • 3.1 reflect on their use of language and differentiate between speech and writing • 3.2 consider how written standard English varies in degrees of formality • 3.3 develop their understanding of the grammar of complex sentences, including clauses and phrases • 3.4 develop their ability to use paragraphs, linking sentences together coherently • 3.5 use the standard written forms of nouns, pronouns, verbs, adjectives, adverbs, prepositions, conjunctions and verb tenses • 3.6 distinguish between words of similar meaning, explain the meanings of words and experiment with choices of vocabulary	Key Grammar provides pupils with activities to: • b present and structure ideas, information and opinions • c observe the different conventions and structures demanded by the various forms of writing • d recognise the function of the paragraph, noticing how it is used in texts that they are reading and use it in their own writing • e use appropriate words needed to discuss their writing, for example, adverb, adjective, paragraph • f observe the conventions of writing and punctuation including grammar and syntax, for example use of the apostrophe to signal omission of a letter or ownership • g use connectives and pronouns appropriately and avoid or reduce repetition and ambiguity in their writing • k set out and punctuate direct speech
2 Using standard English	6.1.S1				
3 Active and passive verbs 1	6.1.S2, 3				
4 Connectives	6.1.S4				
5 Forming complex sentences 1	6.1.S1, 5				
6 Punctuation	6.1.S6				
7 Assessment 1	6.1.S1–6				
8 Active and passive verbs 2	6.2.S1				
9 Official language	6.2.S2				
10 Forming complex sentences 2	6.2.S3				
11 Making notes	6.2.S4				
12 Writing a summary	6.2.S4				
13 Editing	6.2.S4				
14 Conditional sentences	6.2.S5				
15 Assessment 2	6.2.S1–5				
16 Narrative writing	6.3.S1, 3, 4				
17 Past events	6.3.S1, 3, 4				
18 Giving instructions	6.3.S1, 3, 4				
19 Writing reports	6.3.S1, 3, 4				
20 Persuasive writing	6.3.S1, 3, 4				
21 Discussion texts	6.3.S1, 3, 4				
22 Investigating English expressions	6.3.S2				
23 Assessment 3	6.1.S1–6 6.2.S1–5 6.3.S1–4				

Word classes

FOCUS To revise the different word classes: (6.1. S1)
Scottish 5–14: *Adjective, adverb, pronoun* and *conjunction* are categories of words which will be used as pupils discuss with the teacher what they have written

TEACHER INFORMATION

- The terms "conjunction" and "interjection" may be new to some children. Ensure that children have a secure understanding of them. A conjunction is, in fact, a type of connective. When dealing with linking words, it is sometimes better to use the word "connectives" rather than "conjunctions" because we can then include words which are adverbs but which function as linking words, e.g. *so, when* and *where*.
- Because words can belong to more than one class, it is important to emphasise the job that a word does in a sentence.
- Revise ways of determining word class – for example, if it can be changed from singular to plural (or vice versa), it is a noun; if it can be changed from one tense to another, it is a verb.

ANSWERS TO PUPIL'S BOOK

Try it out! *(20 marks)*

1. noun	3. adverb	5. adverb	7. noun	9. noun
2. adjective	4. verb	6. preposition	8. verb	10. noun

11. true
12. true
13. true: "My" in (2), and "Your" in (3)
14. false: "thinks" is a verb
15. true: "Jack" in (5), and "Jill" in (6).

16. true
17. false: only one preposition ("with")
18. false: "please" is an adverb
19. true
20. false: only one preposition ("for")

Keep practising! *(20 marks – 0.5 mark for each correct answer)*

1. himself – pronoun; mistake – noun
2. you – pronoun; them – pronoun
3. careful – adjective; very – adverb
4. Who – pronoun; skilfully – adverb
5. anything – pronoun; tomorrow – adverb

6. left – adverb; next – adjective
7. which – pronoun; box – noun
8. Too – adverb; many – adjective
9. Honesty – noun; best – adjective
10. He – pronoun; tomorrow – noun

11. different
12. me
13. successfully
14. easy, its
15. licence
16. mother, days

17. skilful, an
18. advice, regularly
19. passed, past
20. was, herd
21. Theirs, badly
22. ourselves, but

Take up the challenge! *(20 marks – 0.5 mark for each correct answer)*

1. live – verb; from – preposition
2. Oh – exclamation; me – pronoun
3. flooded – verb; but – connective

4. Who – pronoun; on – preposition
5. usually – adverb; cold – adjective

6–13 Many alternatives are possible, including the following:
6. (verb): think, know, believe; (preposition) in, on, near, by; (proper noun) Mary, Petra, John, Samir
7. (pronoun) Somebody, I; (preposition) under, near, by
8. (exclamation) Oh!, Ah! (adjective) nice, wonderful, marvellous
9. (adverb) recklessly, carelessly, dangerously; (noun) accidents, injuries, deaths
10. (conjunction) but, and, although, so
11. (noun) dogs, cats, elephants; (adjective) good, loving, unsuitable
12. (collective noun) jangle, jumble, jumper
13. (adverb) Suddenly, Quickly, Fearfully; (verb) trapped, locked, living

EXTENSION ACTIVITIES

- Construct or find simple sentences such that pupils can practise replacing the given noun, verb, adjective or adverb with others of their own choosing.
- Similarly, choose simple sentences that do **not** contain adjectives or adverbs. Pupils can insert adjectives or adverbs and consider in what ways they change and/or improve the sentence.
- Children can investigate the occurrence of different word classes in a piece of writing. Which class of word appears most often? Which classes of word are vital to the understanding of a sentence? Which classes of word are easier to change without changing the meaning of the sentence?
- Give each child a copy of PCM1 "Word Classes Cup" (page 56) to complete.

unit 2 Using standard English

FOCUS To revise the conventions of standard English: (6.1. S1)
Scottish 5–14: Purpose and audience will feature regularly when pupils consider what they plan to write or what they have written

TEACHER INFORMATION

- Stress that written language is often different from spoken language. However, take care to ensure that the terms "standard" and "non-standard" are used, rather than "correct" and "incorrect". Children need to know that regional dialects are part of the richness of any language and that there is a time and place when use of such non-standard forms is acceptable.
- In discussing the thorny problem of double negatives, use this explanation to help children understand why "I ain't done nothing wrong" doesn't mean what it appears to!
- If something isn't wrong, it must be right. Then "nothing wrong" means "anything right". Thus the non-standard sentence means "I haven't done anything right" = "I've done something wrong"!

ANSWERS TO PUPIL'S BOOK

Try it out! *(14 marks)*

1. is	4. has	7. were	10. are, is
2. Have	5. is	8. is	11. has
3. is	6. has	9. is	12. is, are

Keep practising! *(8 marks)*

1. she	3. anybody	5. anything	7. am
2. myself	4. Maybe	6. comes	8. anything

Take up the challenge! *(8 marks)*

1. lose her temper/be very angry	5. exhausted/worn out
2. very impressive/striking	6. bored
3. essential/necessary	7. children
4. very popular	8. were very successful

EXTENSION ACTIVITIES

- Encourage pupils to provide examples of errors that they hear or see – and to write them in standard English.
- Encourage pupils to make a list of non-standard words/expressions used in the district of their school or in any other district/region with which they are familiar. Ask them to categorise the words and expressions they have collected.
- Give each child a copy of PCM2 "It's a doddle!" (page 57) to complete.

unit 3

Active and passive verbs 1

FOCUS To understand the terms *active* and *passive* and be able to transform a sentence from one voice to the other: (6.1. S2)
Scottish 5–14: Examining the relationships of words and meanings within sentences

TEACHER INFORMATION

- The word "passive" comes from the Latin word "passus", meaning "suffer" or "undergo". When a verb is passive, the subject could be said to "suffer" the action of the verb (whereas the object "suffers" when the verb is active).
- "Voice" refers to the form of a verb; it is either active or passive.
- Active and passive verb forms include these:

Tense	Active	Passive
Simple Present	*drive(s)*	*is driven*
Present Continuous	*is driving*	*is being driven*
Simple Past	*drove*	*was driven*
Past Continuous	*was driving*	*was being driven*
Present Perfect	*has driven*	*has been driven*
Past Perfect	*had driven*	*had been driven*
Simple Future	*will drive*	*will be driven*

ANSWERS TO PUPIL BOOK

Try it out! *(10 marks)*

1. is blocked
2. are notified
3. is sent
4. are trapped
5. are rescued, (are) taken
6. are put
7. is diverted
8. are questioned
9. are towed
10. are informed

Keep practising! *(10 marks)*

1. was forced
2. was pushed
3. were created
4. were battered
5. were swept
6. were destroyed
7. were killed
8. were buried
9. were found
10. were held

Take up the challenge! *(10 marks)*

1. The barn was struck by lightning.
2. The flying ball hit the referee.
3. The letter was sent by me by email.
4. On Saturday the car was washed and polished by us.
5. Vegetarians do not eat meat.
6. The rain drenched us.
7. The race was won by the slow tortoise.
8. We were kept amazed for hours by the magician.
9. Everyone in our class likes our teacher.
10. The dinner was cooked by me, so the dishes were washed by my brother.

EXTENSION ACTIVITIES

- Pupils can collect examples of passive verbs and investigate **why** a passive verb form has been used. Do passive forms occur more in one type of text than another?
- Children can play an oral game, changing active sentences into passive ones, and vice versa.
- Give each child a copy of PCM3 "Passive verbs" (page 58) to complete.

Connectives

FOCUS   To investigate connecting words and phrases: (6.1. S4)
Scottish 5–14: Examining the relationships of words and meanings within sentences

TEACHER INFORMATION

- The four types of connectives described in the Pupil's Book can be broken down into further categories. For example, the "Cause and effect" connectives might be categorised as follows:

    logic: therefore, thus, hence, consequently, it follows that, it is clear from this
    reason: because, because of, since, as, one reason why, the main reason is
    result: as a result of this, so, so that, therefore, consequently
    This might be an aspect you could develop with more able children.

- Some of the connectives create the type of punctuation problem seen in this common example:

    wrong: We washed the car, then we drove into town.
    right: We washed the car and then we drove into town.
    right: We washed the car. Then we drove into town.
    This problem arises when we use "then", "thus", "therefore" and "(as) for example".

ANSWERS TO PUPIL'S BOOK

Try it out!   *(20 marks)*

1. Although
2. despite the fact that
3. Before that
4. Besides
5. However
6. since
7. as well as
8. because of
9. until
10. unless
11. and then
12 Besides
13. Afterwards
14. In addition, so
15. For example, and, of course
16. so, while

Keep practising!   *(20 marks)*
Alternatives are possible in some cases.

1. while (when, if)
2. because of
3. after (once)
4. However (Unfortunately)
5. Nevertheless (Despite this, In spite of that, However)
6. since (because, as)
7. before (without, instead of)
8. so that (so)
9. although
10. In addition (Furthermore, Also)

11. since; as, In addition, Also
12. Soon; because
13. So, Therefore, As a result; in spite of
14. After, Subsequent to; Consequently, Therefore
15. While; Additionally, In addition

Take up the challenge!   *(20 marks)*
Alternative answers are possible.
(1 mark for each correct answer)

1. However
2. On the other hand, Nevertheless
3. that
4. Subsequently

5. then, but first

8. Moreover

6. Beside, Although

9. For example, Similarly

7. – (All are suitable.)

10. instead of

(2 marks for each correct answer)

11. This is the house where we used to live.
12. When our family grew very big, the house became too small for us.
   Our family grew so big that the house became too small for us.
13. The new house that my parents bought was very expensive.
   My parents bought a new house, which was very expensive.
14. We hired a lorry so that we could move everything ourselves and reduce the cost.
15. Paul hurt his left arm when he was helping to lift the piano into the lorry.

EXTENSION ACTIVITIES

- Children could look at texts relating to topics they are studying in other subjects, and consider the connectives used in specific subjects such as maths, science and history. Do certain types of connectives feature in certain types of writing and certain subjects?

- Children could listen to, or record, a conversation between two people and write down the connectives used in speech that we don't often use in writing – e.g. *Well, As a matter of fact, It seems to me, It looks as if, Never mind, I'm not sure but I think.*

- Give each child a copy of PCM4 "Connectives crossword" (page 59) to complete.

unit 5

Forming complex sentences 1

FOCUS   To practise forming complex sentences: (6.1. S5)
Scottish 5–14: Sentence structures can be discussed in terms of how they create
meaning, mood and atmosphere

TEACHER INFORMATION

- A participle (–ing word) can be a verb, an adjective or part of a compound
  noun.
    adjective: *We are going on a walking tour in August.*
    verb: *Look! The baby is walking.*
    noun: *Where is my walking-stick?*
- Sentences starting with a present participle can often be ambiguous. For
  example: *Getting out of the car, we saw an elderly lady.* Who was getting out of the
  car: the speaker or the elderly lady? It could be rewritten as: *As we were getting
  out of the car, we saw an elderly lady* or *We saw an elderly lady getting out of the car.*
- The complexity of sentences in a child's writing is an indication of his or her
  writing development. Encourage children continually to proofread their own
  writing and to look for ways they can combine simple sentences to give their
  writing more variety and cohesion.

ANSWERS TO PUPIL'S BOOK

Try it out!   *(10 marks)*
1. Anita opened the box, thinking that it was empty.
2. No comma needed.
3. I started to put on a shoe, believing that it was mine.
4. No comma needed.
5. No comma needed.
6. Joseph opened the door, not realising that his father was painting the other side of it.
7. I picked up the wallet, wondering whether the owner's name was inside it.
8. No comma needed.
9. No comma needed.
10. Gordon sat in a cell at the police station, bitterly regretting his night out.

Keep practising!   *(10 marks)*
1. After we had finished lunch, Mary and I cleared the table.
2. After the dentist had taken a tooth out, Paul's mouth felt numb for hours.
3. Although cows are big animals, they do not normally attack people.
4. Although ice-cream and chocolate may not be very good for you, I like them both.
5. Despite the fact that Scotland can be a very chilly place, we are very happy living there.
6. Despite the fact that John is not very tall, he is an excellent soccer player.
   Despite John's lack of height, he is an excellent soccer player.
7. Because of the ice on the road, it has been closed to traffic.
8. Because of their very thick skin, crocodiles are not easily injured.
9. Before we went to bed, we turned off all the lights.
10. Before he went for a ride with his friend, Ranjeet checked the brakes on his bike.
    Ranjeet checked the brakes on his bike before he went for a ride with his friend.

Take up the challenge!   *(10 marks)*

Open-ended. Examples are:
1. What's the name of the girl who sits next to Susan?
2. The player who scored the winning goal used to go to our school.
3. What have you done with the video that we rented?
4. The shop that caught fire is a complete wreck, so it will have to be rebuilt.
5. The police are trying to find out who was driving the car.
6. Did you ever find out the name of the woman whose dog bit you?
7. The team which wins on Saturday will go through to the final.
8. The candidate whom I nominated has won the election.
9. The answer that my friend got was different from mine.
10. Can you please tell me what I did wrong?

EXTENSION ACTIVITIES

- Start with a simple sentence and ask pupils to do one of these things:
  - add a given type of clause e.g. adverbial of time, adjectival, adverbial of condition and so on;
  - add a clause starting with a particular word (e.g. *although, if, when*) or type of word (e.g. a present participle).
- Children can look at texts, pick out interesting complex sentences and identify the main and subordinate clauses.
- Give each child a copy of PCM5, "Sort them out!" (page 60) to complete.

Punctuation

FOCUS To revise and extend knowledge and use of punctuation marks: (6.1. S6)
Scottish 5–14: Checking punctuation, linkage and organization will be part of the process of redrafting at this stage

TEACHER INFORMATION

- Semi-colons, colons, brackets and dashes are difficult items of punctuation to use. In many cases, their use is a matter of judgement and personal preference. Encourage children to "have a go" in their own writing, ensuring that you then take the time to discuss with them how and why they've made a particular decision. Pupils can be helped to understand the use of brackets, dashes and parenthetical expressions but only the most able ones can be expected to use them at this level.

ANSWERS TO PUPIL'S BOOK

Try it out! *(10 marks)*

1. Please give this book to Mike when you see him. It is from his uncle in Wales.
2. We put all our bags in the boot of the car. Then we set off on our journey, looking forward to visiting our relatives in Cornwall.
3. Although the crowd was very noisy and shouted insults at some of the visiting players, there was no serious disturbance. This was a pleasant surprise for the police.
4. That's Kate's brother. Come and meet him. He plays in goal for his school team.
5. Sri Lanka is an island country off the southern tip of India. It used to be called Ceylon.
6. "Thanks for the camera," Kate said to her uncle. "It will be very useful."
7. The woman asked me what my name is and where I live.
8. I'm not sure how much Margaret paid for her new bicycle.
9. You can throw those old shoes away. They're no good now.
10. We waited a few minutes. Then we went round to the back of the house.

(10 marks – 2 marks for each correct sentence)

11. Use two of these words in your own sentences: through, across, around, into, beyond.
12. The traffic in front of us came to a halt; we guessed that there had been an accident.
13. That cat is not ours; it belongs to one of our neighbours.
14. Mrs Wilson glanced at the items on her shopping list: milk, tea, sugar, cereal and fruit.
15. No change.

Keep practising! *(20 marks)*

1. Mary's (possession)
2. game's (omission); minutes' (possession)
3. She's (omission); Grandma's (possession)
4. There's (omission); neighbour's or neighbours'(possession)
5. Let's (omission); Peter's (possession); I'm (omission); won't (omission)
6. Paul's; Anne's (possession)
7. children's (possession); there's (omission)
8. Who's (omission); plumber's or plumbers' (possession)
9. Mike's (possession); else's (possession)
10. people's (possession); judges' (possession); isn't (omission)

11. Mrs Collins, the librarian, told us to be quiet.
12. Her colourful Mexican hat had red, green, blue and yellow stripes on it.
13. Ahmed broke through the winner's tape at the end of the race, shouting 'I'm the champion!'
14. Encouraged by the crowd's shouts, the players, who hadn't won a game for weeks, were spurred on to victory.

15. When my granny's teeth fell into her soup, we shrieked with laughter!
16. "Won't you please turn that noise down?" pleaded my dad.
17. Since the new puppy's arrival, there's never a dull moment in our house.
18. The tiger, which had escaped from the zoo, was stalking Ann's pony.
19. "I don't believe it!" she gasped. "There's an elephant sitting on my car!"
20. Doesn't your friend live near Buckingham Palace in London?

Take up the challenge!

(20 marks – 2 marks for each correctly written sentence)
Open-ended. The decision as to whether the pupil opts for commas, brackets or dashes is a personal one. As long as the correct phrases (listed below) are separated and the punctuation is accurate, award full marks.
1. unaware of the approaching storm
2. two boys and two girls
3. but not by any means the only problem
4. but not her brother
5. 9 o'clock our time
6. the main witness for the prosecution
7. and even if you can't
8. which he admitted; which he denied *(nb: the punctuation should be the same for both)*
9. like many other things
10. the chief executive's personal secretary; or the most important part of it *(nb: the punctuation does not need to be the same for these)*

EXTENSION ACTIVITIES

- Ask children to find further examples of one or more of the punctuation marks, including examples which contain possible mistakes of punctuation. Then discuss them in class.
- Children could write their own unpunctuated sentences for other pupils to punctuate.
- Give each child a copy of PCM6 "Punctuation posers" (page 61) to complete.

unit 7 Assessment 1

ANSWERS TO PUPIL'S BOOK

Word class quiz *(5 marks – 0.5 mark for each correct answer)*

1. Madrid
2. interesting/exciting
3. themselves
4. congregation
5. well
6. biggest/largest
7. through
8. also/furthermore/besides
9. begun
10. dying

Make a choice 1 *(5 marks – 0.5 mark for each correct answer)*

1. worse
2. silent
3. an
4. a
5. than
6. p
7. or
8. anything
9. effect
10. me

Make a choice 2 *(5 marks – 0.5 mark for each correct answer)*

1. since
2. successfully
3. its
4. Practice
5. ours
6. are
7. has
8. past, it
9. X
10. caused, evidence

Make a choice 3 *(5 marks – 0.5 mark for each correct answer)*

1. saw
2. broken
3. stolen, sold
4. forget
5. grounds, blown
6. an, but, a
7. a, an
8. an, a
9. Does, Mike's
10. have *(because of "their")*

Make a choice 4 *(10 marks)*

1. and then, passed
2. and therefore, Friday
3. Besides, hardly
4. However, it
5. finishing, giving

Using passive verbs *(10 marks – 1 mark for each correct answer)*

1. is held
2. is marked
3. is given
4. are invited
5. are often used

6. was won
7. was wearing
8. was broken
9. was printed
10. was given

Joining sentences *(10 marks – 2 marks for each correct sentence)*
Alternatives are possible.

1. These are the best of the photos (that/which) Uncle Amos took with his new camera last summer.
2. Many trains and a large number of buses were delayed by a severe storm lasting nearly 48 hours.
3. We put sandbags in front of our door, hoping that they would stop the water from coming in, but they were not completely successful.
4. Yesterday Anne hurt her left leg when she was playing on the trampoline, but the doctor says the injury is not serious.
5. The shop that used to sell fireworks has stopped selling them because parents and the police complained that very young children were able to buy them.

Punctuating sentences *(10 marks – 2 marks for each correct sentence)*
Alternatives are possible.

1. Paul checked the email on Mary's computer. Then he turned it off because he wanted to phone his friend and arrange to go fishing with him.
2. Although Sophie is not a strong swimmer, she rescued a young girl at the swimming-pool and stayed with her while she recovered. Then she escorted her home.

3. "There's something wrong with the printer," Mike told his father. "It won't print."
   "Check to see if there's any paper in it," his father said. "You may have to put some paper in."
4. The notice on the door of Mr Singh's shop was quite clear. "CLOSED," it said in capital letters. "Open 1–5 p.m.," it added in small letters.
5. Dave Burton, the captain of our team, scored twice in the first half. Then he pulled a muscle in his left leg, so Mr Donald replaced him at half-time by sending on John Lee, our reserve striker.

unit 8 · Active and passive verbs 2

FOCUS To understand the terms *active* and *passive* and be able to transform a sentence from one voice to the other: (6.2. S1)

Scottish 5–14: Examining the relationships of words and meanings within sentences

TEACHER INFORMATION

- Ensure children understand the changes involved when sentences are altered from the active to the passive voice: the subject is put after the verb. The verb has a word like "is" or "was" added to it, and the word "by" is added after the verb.
- Although the word "by" followed by the "agent" (doer) is often a useful indicator of the passive voice, the agent may be omitted and the sentence will still make sense: e.g. *The missing clues were found.* In such cases, the agent is usually implicit from the context. For example, in a science report about a medical experiment, the agent of the sentence "Each patient was given a tablet" is whoever was conducting the experiment.

ANSWERS TO PUPIL'S BOOK

Try it out! *(10 marks – 2 marks for each correct sentence)*
Passive present verbs: are manufactured, are assembled, are made, are imported, are advertised
Passive past verbs: were produced, were exported, was used, were made, were closed

Keep practising! *(10 marks – 0.5 mark for each correct answer)*
1. is boiled, is drunk
2. are destroyed, are killed
3. are lost, is sunk, is hit
4. were invited, was held, were asked
5. are made, is inspected, is tested
6. were built, was provided, was opened
7. are weighed, are examined
8. were established, were disqualified

Take up the challenge! *(10 marks – 2 marks for each correct sentence)*
1. Your watch was found in the playground this afternoon by Tanya.
2. A professional chef cooked the food.
3. Our computer was repaired by an expert a few days ago.
4. Security officials searched all the passengers on the flight.
5. Two men have been arrested by the police and taken to the police station.

EXTENSION ACTIVITIES

- Children can search texts for passive verbs, including ones in sentences where the agent is omitted. Consider what is achieved by using passive (rather than active) verb forms. List the reasons why writers sometimes use passive (rather than active) verb forms.
- Give each child a copy of PCM7 "Recount of an earthquake"(page 62) to complete.

unit 9 Official language

FOCUS To understand the features of formal official language: (6.1. S2)
Scottish 5–14: Examining the relationships of words and meanings within sentences

TEACHER INFORMATION

- The term "register" in grammar refers to the way a particular situation, audience and topic affect the language in a text. The social context of a text determines whether it is formal or informal, personal or impersonal.
- In the past 20 or 30 years, the Government and many business firms have tried to use plain, simple English in an effort to be more "customer friendly".
- A good source of official language is almost any legal document, including the small print in agreements concerning money, e.g. mortgage agreements. Point out that the (often complex) sentences in small print have been approved by solicitors and are often very involved to provide a legal defence.

ANSWERS TO PUPIL'S BOOK

Try it out! *(10 marks)*

1. communicate directly with
2. a proposed short-term lease
3. It is our understanding
4. take temporary possession of
5. a period not exceeding seven calendar days
6. you indicate your consent
7. employ your best efforts
8. on one and the same occasion
9. adverse structural change, deterioration of parts or other harmful effects
10. delivering (it)

Keep practising! *(10 marks)*

Award marks flexibly for correctly translating and communicating the main points, for example:
It's an amusing letter from Len about lending me his bicycle. He has invented a firm of solicitors who want me to agree that, when Len lends me his bike for a week, I will agree to pay for any damage, not let more than three people on the bike together, and return the bike on time.

Take up the challenge! *(10 marks)*

1. Please note
2. We think/believe
3. Do you agree to pay for any damage?
4. The agreement will end on …
5. His account of the event is untrue.
6. He was driving recklessly.
7. He is likely to get a lot of money if he auctions his land.
8. He was accused of stealing.
9. She is a conceited young lady.
10. You must be silent (not talk) in a library.

EXTENSION ACTIVITIES

- Children can collect examples of formal notices and documents.(Asking parents is a good starting point.). They can look for recurring formal expressions and make a list of these with their "translations".
- Children can try writing their own "contract" for some negotiation they are having with a friend or family member.
- Find real opportunities to write formal letters. If, for example, there is a local issue or proposal that is being debated, children could write to a councillor expressing their views.
- Children could carry out research to find out about the Plain English Campaign.
- Give each child a copy of PCM8 "What does it mean?" (page 63) to complete.

Forming complex sentences 2

FOCUS To revise and extend work on clauses and complex sentences: (6.1. S3)
Scottish 5–14: Sentence structures can be discussed in terms of how they create meaning, mood and atmosphere

TEACHER INFORMATION

- Remind pupils of the difference between compound sentences and complex sentences. Compound sentences contain two main clauses. Complex sentences contain a main clause and one or more subordinate clauses.

- Although the aim of this unit is to develop children's ability to write more sophisticated, complex sentences, it should be remembered that there is sometimes a need to teach them to shorten (rather than to lengthen) their sentences.

- The different types of clauses (adverbial, adjectival and noun) become easier to understand if pupils have a sound knowledge of the function of adverbs, adjectives and nouns.

ANSWERS TO PUPIL'S BOOK

Try it out!   *(20 marks)*
1. Our game was cancelled
2. he still plays football for a local team.
3. What's the name of the player
4. Our dog barks
5. The grass has turned brown
6. The bus takes me straight to school
7. you will probably feel tired the next day.
8. The watch belongs to Sarjit Singh.
9. The bus was full
10. the starter won't fire his gun.

11. who is caught stealing from a shop
12. so that we get enough fresh air.
13. who knows Mary Wilson
14. As soon as the water boils
15. where nobody else would ever think of looking.
16. that I borrowed from the library
17. whose name I read out
18. Once Sadie had learned to swim
19. when you go into the hospital.
20. for which Tom plays

Keep practising!   *(20 marks)*
Alternatives are possible. Examples are:
1. *If* you want to go with us, you must be ready in five minutes.
2. No one expected our team to win *because* they'd not won a game all season.
3. *As soon as* the shopkeeper lowered his prices, his sales increased.
4. He tried his best *but* it wasn't good enough.
5. *Whatever* the problem, you can count on me to help.
6. They came to a stop *where* the road forked in three directions.
7. We could hear perfectly *although* we were in the last row.
8. The candidate, *who* campaigned tirelessly, unfortunately lost.
9. *After* I received the hoax phone call, I notified the police.

10. The city *that* I love the most is Paris.
11. When the referee blows his whistle, the players will leave the field.
12. I want to get the autograph of the player who scored the winning goal.
13. The police are trying to find out what caused the accident.
14. What was the name of the ice cream you bought last week?
15. If there is a drought, water will be rationed.
16. Mel put a stamp on the envelope and then posted it.
   After Mel had put a stamp on the envelope, she posted it.
17. Samir wants to know how much a mobile phone costs.
18. That's the boy whose father used to be a boxer.
19. There was dense fog this morning, so there were a number of minor accidents.
20. Show me the photos that you took during the holidays.

Take up the challenge! *(20 marks)*

1–10: Award 0.5 mark for each correctly identified type of clause and 0.5 mark for each sentence ending that is logical and appropriate. Answers will vary, but examples are:

1. The committee could not agree, so the chairperson cast the deciding vote. (subordinate)
2. Unless the weather is bad, the game will take place. (main)
3. Whatever you say, I can't believe she is innocent. (main)
4. Encouraged by his coach, the tennis player turned professional. (main)
5. Our teacher said we could have a disco, if we arranged it all ourselves. (subordinate)
6. So that no one gets hurt, please use a safety net. (main)
7. We waited ages for the taxi. Mum was not very happy. (subordinate)
8. Whenever I feel afraid, I whistle a happy tune. (main)
9. Joseph was sleeping soundly while all around him there was chaos. (subordinate)
10. Before we had time to think, we were agreeing to everything. (main)

11–15: Award 2 marks for each sentence correctly analysed.

Main clause	Subordinate clause	Subordinate clause type
11. she is a very fast runner	Although Susan is not very tall	adverbial
12. I know the woman	who won the lottery jackpot	adjectival
13. Call me	when you are ready to leave	adverbial
14. We told the woman	what she wanted to know	noun
15. Don't eat the cheese	that I bought for the party	adjectival

EXTENSION ACTIVITIES

- Children can try to complete the same main-clause sentence starter in different ways using different connectives – for example: *We waited for the bus because we didn't want to walk; We waited for the bus although we were already late; We waited for the bus after our car broke down.*

- Children can select a page of text from a book and investigate what type of sentence each sentence is, whether clauses are main or subordinate, and, if subordinate, what type.

- Give each child a copy of PCM 9 "Investigating clauses" (page 64) to complete.

Making notes

FOCUS To contract sentences and develop note-making skills: (6.2. S4)
Scottish 5–14: Purpose and audience will feature regularly when pupils consider what they plan to write or what they have written

TEACHER INFORMATION

- Try to find as many realistic opportunities and reasons as you can to encourage children to make notes. Remind children that notes do not have to be complete words or sentences.
- One of the problems that can occur with note-making is that we abbreviate and shorten to such an extent that the notes become ambiguous or meaningless. Developing a "shorthand" of our own often helps.

ANSWERS TO PUPIL'S BOOK

Try it out!   *(10 marks)*
Answers will vary slightly, depending on the individual pupil.
1. In the space for 21st November: X's birthday.
2. In the space for lst August: Dentist, me, 10.30.
3. In the space for 6th August: Holiday Spain till 14 Aug. Leave by noon.
   In the space for 14th August: Return from holiday.
4. In the space for 10th May: Sue's party. 5–9 pm, Rm 3 Mem Hall, Market St.
5. In the space for 6th June: 4.30 pm, optician, me.

Keep practising!   *(10 marks)*
Answers will vary. Award marks flexibly. Examples are:
1. Doris, Newton Motors, Mrs J – car ready for collection, 8-8 any day. (received 4.30 p.m.)
2. Mrs J – Receptionist rang re appt Dr Jordan 8 March. Can't do. Re-scheduled 10.30, 10 March. If no good, phone 094-384 (received 4.50 p.m.)

Take up the challenge!   *(10 marks)*
Answers will vary. Award marks flexibly for appropriate selection of information and note-making style. Examples are:
1. Tom Logan, ser accid M99, 2 miles S j38 – lorry v. petr-tanker, fire, road blocked both ways, 2 cars into wreck, 2 amb required, firemen needed, traffic stopped.
2. Cynthia Marsden 48 Larch St. 2 men ? breaking into rear 44 Larch St, carrying goods to van in lane behind houses, susp burglars.

EXTENSION ACTIVITIES

- Give pairs of children a scenario (e.g. a job interview) where one has to interview the other and take notes.
- Children can try to reconstruct messages or texts from notes that other children have written. Or they could try to write a well-known story in note form and see if someone else can tell what it is.
- Ask children to develop a "Note-making Dictionary", containing high-frequency words and shortened forms or abbreviations for them – e.g. *re* (regarding, about); *rtn* (return); *b'day* (birthday); *appt* (appointment).
- Ask children to look at classified adverts in local newspapers to see how items for sale are described in note form.
- Give each child a copy of PCM10 "Call the Coastguard!" (page 65) to complete.

unit 12 Writing a summary

FOCUS To contract sentences and develop summarising skills: (6.2. S4)
Scottish 5–14: *Main point, topic sentence* and *evidence* are aspects of texts to which pupils will now give attention in their writing

TEACHER INFORMATION

- Summarising is a useful way of understanding and remembering something that is said or read. Encourage pupils to make summaries of non-fiction texts they are reading in other subjects of the curriculum. Suggest the following procedure:
  - Read the text.
  - Identify the main ideas.
  - List the important details you remember.
  - Scan the text to make sure you've included all important details.
  - Review your list – get rid of non-essential points.
  - Begin summary by stating main idea, then write a sentence or two for each important detail.

ANSWERS TO PUPIL'S BOOK

Try it out! *(10 marks)*

1. farm	3. class	5. crowd	7. through	9. team
2. Parliament	4. present	6. increase	8. orchestra	10. navy

Keep practising! *(10 marks)*
Some of the answers may be a matter of opinion.

1. a) appropriate	b) inappropriate	c) inappropriate	
2. a) inappropriate	b) appropriate	c) inappropriate	
3. a) appropriate	b) inappropriate	c) inappropriate	d) inappropriate

Take up the challenge! *(10 marks – 2.5 marks for each suitable summary)*
1. Pope John Paul II died in 2005 after a lengthy illness.
2. Last month Mary had influenza and was absent for nearly a week.
3. Paul's brother was hurt playing football but helped his team to win 2–1.
4. I am happy that next month we will move to a house nearer school.

EXTENSION ACTIVITIES

- It is helpful to pupils to do the opposite of making a summary, i.e. by taking a simple sentence (with subject, verb and object) and by enlarging it by doing some or all of the following:
  - giving more information about the subject, action or object;
  - adding irrelevant information;
  - using repetition;
  - adding negative pieces of information.
- This type of work makes pupils more aware of what they have to omit when making a summary.
- Give pupils articles cut from newspapers without their headlines. Pupils can then read the articles and write their own headlines.
- Give each pupil a copy of PCM11 "The Wickham Rainbow" (page 66) to complete.

Editing

FOCUS To develop editing skills: (6.2. S4)
Scottish 5–14: Checking punctuation, linkage and organization will be part of the process of redrafting at this stage

TEACHER INFORMATION

- In editing, the first job is to see whether the layout, length and approach of the material are in accordance with the situation (including the intended market or reader) and any instructions given.
- In real life, we would need to know the role of the editor. Does he/she have the power to make such changes as seem appropriate, or must he/she keep closely to the author's text? A newspaper editor usually reserves the right to make whatever changes seem desirable. On the other hand, in publishing, some editors can make suggestions to an author but not change anything without the author's consent.
- Editing involves both content and the techniques needed for presentation, e.g. spelling, punctuation, grammar, vocabulary and layout.

ANSWERS TO PUPIL'S BOOK

Try it out! *(10 marks)*
1. Paul found a watch in the playground. It looked like his friend's, so he went to find him.
2. "Dave," Paul said. "Is this yours? I was going to take it to the school office, but I thought I'd better ask you first."
3. David was astonished because he had not even noticed that his watch was missing. He looked at his wrist. Then he took the watch and examined it carefully.
4. "Yes, it's definitely mine," David said. "Where did you find it? I don't remember taking it off."
5. "In the playground," Paul told him. "It was lying on the ground near Miss Smith's car. Have you been near her car this morning?"
6. "I'm not sure," David said. "Ah! Now I remember," he added. "We were playing a game near the cars, and John grabbed me by the arm. It must have come off then."

Keep practising! *(10 marks – 0.5 mark for each correct answer)*

1. those; their	6. gone; until
2. beginning; improved	7. sergeant; trial
3. address; forgotten	8. receipt; guarantee
4. are going; develop	9. mischievous; tail
5. quite; exciting	10. felt; embarrassed

Take up the challenge! *(10 marks)*
The effectiveness of the piece could be improved in many ways: e.g. "got" could be replaced once or twice in sentence 4; "nice" could be replaced by another word in sentence 7; more variety of sentence construction, etc. Award marks flexibly. The specific spelling, grammar and punctuation errors are:

Sentence 1: overseas, works	Sentence 7: school. It
Sentence 3: work; woke	Sentence 8: returned home; hour
Sentence 4: of bed; washed. Then	Sentence 9: weather
Sentence 5: friends	Sentence 12: replied to some
Sentence 6: lessons	Sentence 14: tired, so

EXTENSION ACTIVITIES

- Pupils could discuss the responsibilities and powers that professional editors have e.g. what changes can you make without consulting the author? What will happen if you want to change the wording of a sentence but the author does not agree with you?
- Present pupils with texts and a range of scenarios in which they have to act as editors. For example, present them with a page from one of the Harry Potter books. Tell them they have recently been appointed as editor in the company that publishes the Harry Potter books. How would they edit the page? Or present them with a newspaper article. What would they do with it as a news sub-editor?
- Give each child a copy of PCM12 "Editing" (page 67) to complete.

unit 14 Conditional sentences

FOCUS To investigate and use conditional sentences: (6.2. S5)
Scottish 5–14: *Clause* is an element which will now feature in discussion of sentence structure

TEACHER INFORMATION

- Conditional clauses are used to talk about possible situations and their consequences. If the conditional clause comes at the beginning of the sentence, there should be a comma before the main clause (as in this sentence!).
- In the pattern *"If + Simple Past tense + would/might/could"* (showing unlikely or impossible actions), we use the subjunctive form "were" (instead of "was") with all subjects – singular or plural.

ANSWERS TO PUPIL'S BOOK

Try it out! *(20 marks)*
1–15 (15 marks)

1. f	6. o	11. d
2. a	7. l	12. g
3. k	8. c	13. j
4. i	9. h	14. m
5. n	10. b	15. e

Award 1 mark for each of children's own sentences (5 marks)

Keep practising! *(20 marks)*

1. could	7. liked; would be
2. may	8. might have
3. will	9. have been; didn't
4. would; might	10. used; would
5. pays; were; would	11. would have
6. don't; could	12. lived; would

Take up the challenge! *(20 marks)*
1–6 (9 marks)

1. had not stopped; have been killed	4. had fallen; have got
2. have hit	5. had not fallen
3. have had	6. had taken; would have been

7–9 (6 marks)

7. Tom could have bought some fish and chips if the shop had not been closed.
8. If the bus had not broken down, Anne would not have been late for school.
9. If Susan and the lifeguard had not saved the children, they would have (been) drowned.

10–14 (5 marks)
Open-ended. Award marks for grammatically correct answers.

EXTENSION ACTIVITIES

- Encourage pupils to create scenarios similar to that of Mr Trant in "Take up the challenge!" in the Pupil's Book, and then to make up relevant "if" sentences about it.
- Children read the poem "If" by Rudyard Kipling, which is one long conditional sentence! They could then try to write an "If" poem of their own.
- Give each pupil a copy of PCM13 "What if?" (page 68) to complete.

Assessment 2

ANSWERS TO PUPIL'S BOOK

NB: In many cases, alternative answers are possible.

From active to passive *(5 marks – 0.5 mark for each correct sentence)*
1. Our car is being repaired today.
2. The car was still being repaired at half past five
3. Leah was praised for her bravery in rescuing a drowning child.
4. Miss Fisher's car was damaged in a car park yesterday.
5. Many people are injured in traffic accidents each month.
6. The factory opposite Ravi's home has been damaged by a major fire.
7. Several new houses have been built on land near our school.
8. Linda has been chosen to play netball for our school team.
9. The police say the two robbers will soon be caught.
10. The men will be arrested and charged with assault and robbery.

Choosing verb forms *(10 marks)*
1. found; is thinking
2. received; have been
3. are made; are imported
4. would … reply; can
5. is getting; have been invited

Joining sentences *(10 marks)*
1. Although Claire did not like the taste of the medicine, she managed to swallow two spoonfuls of it.
2. It was getting dark, so Charlie switched on the light in the kitchen.
3. Birds avoid the berries of some plants because they know that they are poisonous, although they are very pretty.
4. What's the name of the shop in Bond Road that sells parts for our printer?
5. That's the name of the man who nearly caught the thief who stole his car yesterday.
6. Ashra won the race although she was wearing tight running shoes borrowed from a friend because she had forgotten to bring her own running shoes.
7. The camera was so expensive that Alex decided not to buy it.
   The camera was very expensive, so Alex decided not to buy it.
8. My cousin, the manager of a computer company, has taught us how to use computers to research topics for our work at school. (so that we can research)
9. We had to wait a few minutes because the food was so hot that we could not eat it immediately. (too hot for us to eat)
10. The girls said they were Swiss tourists staying here with friends for a fortnight.

Finding the main clause *(10 marks)*
1. Any runner … may be disqualified
2. Ask the lady … or …
3. That's the shop
4. the price of petrol has reached record heights recently
5. We're ready to leave
6. The only reason … is your age
7. You can borrow my book … Sue
8. I don't know much about farm animals
9. I can easily shorten them for you … Mary
10. The doctor told Peter

Making notes (*10 marks– 5 marks for each set of notes*)

The notes need not contain complete words or expressions because the way in which they are made depends very largely on the person who makes them. However, they should obviously and accurately reflect the important details of the phone conversations. Examples are:

1. Mrs W: Janet Middleton, mother, cancel mtg tomor, husband toothache – dentist. Will phone tomor aft/eve re new mtg. Don't worry. (recd: 5.20)

2. Mr W: Tony Ellis, Stockton Ellis est agt. Phone bk bef 7 –044-342 – or tomor off 084-597 re buyer for Bank St prop – decision needed asap.

Using connectives (*5 marks – 0.5 mark for each correct answer*)

1. unless	3. Although	5. than	7. despite	9. before
2. if	4. since	6. which	8. so that/so	10. when

Writing summaries (*10 marks– 5 marks for each summary*)

Answers will vary. Examples are:

1. There's a good film about Scotland on television Channel 4 at 8 p.m. tonight.

2. House martins nest under the eaves of our house from April to September every year.

Narrative writing

FOCUS To investigate some of the key features of narrative texts: (6.3. S1)
Scottish 5–14: Sentence structures using good models from pupils' reading can be
discussed in terms of how they create meaning, mood and atmosphere. Direct
speech and ways of indicating it can be taught by looking at texts read

TEACHER INFORMATION

- A narrative text is one that re-tells events, often in chronological order. Usually,
the purpose of narrative texts, which can be prose or poetry, is to entertain. At
this stage children should be familiar with narrative form. This unit focuses
specifically on the use of language (for example, effective choice of descriptive
words and connectives) and sentence structures (for example, direct speech,
variety of simple, compound and complex sentences).

ANSWERS TO PUPIL'S BOOK

Answers will vary in some cases. Appropriate examples are given.

Try it out! *(20 marks)*
1. He starts with a statement to introduce and then describe his sister, Mrs Gargery. *(1 mark)*
2. Two main clauses: a) My siser, Mrs Joe Gargery, was more than twenty years older than me; b)
   (and) had established a great reputation with the neighbours.
   One subordinate clause: because she had brought me up "by hand" *(2 marks)*
3. Mrs Joe: a hard and heavy hand; not a good-looking woman; black hair and eyes; a red skin;
   bony
   Joe Gargery: a fair man; flaxen hair; smooth face; blue eyes; mild, good-natured, sweet-
   tempered, easy-going, foolish dear fellow *(3 marks)*
4. He uses "peeped" to show that Pip is frightened. "Fenced" tells us that Joe Gargery felt
   protective towards Pip. *(2 marks)*
5. He called the news "dismal" because he was afraid that his sister would hit him with the cane.
   Other descriptive words include *fellow-sufferer, peeped, miserably, crying* and *rubbing myself. (3 marks)*
6. I asked: nervously, timidly, quickly; repeated my sister: angrily, fiercely, tersely, indignantly; I said:
   humbly, cautiously, nervously *(3 marks)*
7. It is an example of direct speech. Written as reported speech it would be: I asked Joe if (my
   sister) had been gone long. *(3 marks)*
8. It is written in the first person. We can tell this from the first word, "My", and the use of "me"
   in the same sentence. This use makes the story more realistic, credible and immediate. *(3 marks)*

Keep practising! *(20 marks)*
1. It is written in the first person ("we", "our") and the past tense ("approached"; "led",
   "drifted").
   (1 mark)
2. sight: *glare of lights; coloured bulbs; eerie darkness; luminous spiders*
   hearing: *murmur of the crowd; sizzling hotdogs; mysterious groans and wailing*
   smell: *pungent smell of sizzling hotdogs and sweet candyfloss; exhaust fumes surrounded us*
   taste: *sweet candyfloss, bitter flavour coated our tongues*
   touch: *hard, wooden seats, steel-cold restraining bar (10 marks)*
3. He uses a semi-colon after "crowd" because the following statement is linked closely to the
   preceding one. *(2 marks)*
4. We could hear the murmur of the crowd *and* see the coloured bulbs on the stalls. All roads led
   to the Fair *and* they were all packed with people. *(2 marks)*
5. As we *gradually* approached; *brilliantly* reflected in the sky; *immediately* swallowed up *(3 marks)*
6. It was with great relief that we saw the exit appear in the distance. *(2 marks)*

Take up the challenge! *(20 marks)*

1. The author uses a dash to give us time to think about the problem. *(2 marks)*
2. Examples include *playing around; oodles of 'em; Must of; could take them all on; wipe the floor with; We were just out for a walk, right; in me life; I ain't thrown nothing at nobody.* The words and expressions are used to create the realism of spoken language. *(4 marks)*
3. He changes from a past to a present tense in lines 2 and 8. He does this when a sentence or remark is not part of the past action but is a comment inserted by the present narrator. *(3 marks)*
4. The use of "parlour" implies that this incident occurred some years ago when "parlour" was used instead of "lounge" or "living-room". The parlour was the best room; it was reserved for special occasions and for receiving guests formally. *(3 marks)*
5. *CRASH!* – The author uses capital letters to emphasise the loudness of the noise. *(3 marks)*
6. *when, until, then, finally, By the time* *(5 marks)*

EXTENSION ACTIVITIES

- Read to children (or let them read it themselves) the part in *Great Expectations* by Charles Dickens that follows on from the adapted extract given in the Pupil's Book.
- Children could write continuations of either (or both) of the extracts "The fun of the fair" or "Ken and the potato" given in the Pupil's Book. The writing should be in keeping with the style of the originals.
- Children can investigate other examples of narrative text, looking for examples of the language features highlighted in this Unit.
- Give each child a copy of PCM14 "The war against the moles" (page 69) to complete.

unit
17

Describing past events

FOCUS To revise some of the language features of recounts: (6.3. S1)
Scottish 5–14: Paragraphing and other text features can be developed by making clear the link with the purpose of writing.

TEACHER INFORMATION

- A recount text is one that retells past events, often in chronological order, for the purpose of information or entertainment. At this stage children should be familiar with recount form, if not the actual term. This Unit focuses on characteristic features such as orientation of the piece in terms of time and place; the use of past tense verbs, both active and passive; and time connectives to give the text cohesion.

ANSWERS TO PUPIL'S BOOK

Try it out! *(25 marks)*
1. It tells what happened when a bull elephant charged a moving passenger train in Malaya. *(2 marks)*
2. *Any four of these:* When, and then, In an instant, Eventually, In the end, shortly after. *(4 marks)*
3. The important thing in this account is the railway line and not who built it, so the writer has put the more important thing first. *(1 mark)*
4. was built, was expected, were taken, was buried, (was) put up *(4 marks)*
5. a) The events were the charge of the elephant and the derailment of the train.*(1 mark)*
   b) Here, "him" was the driver of the train. *(1 mark)*
   c) He was wrong in thinking that there was no threat to the train. *(1 mark)*
6. Charging bull derails train. *(1 mark)*

The 10 mistakes in the report are: are pulling – were pulling; all together – altogether; While – When; nor – or; Soon – As soon as/When; begins – began; hits – hit; were – was; damage – damaged; report – reported. *(10 marks)*

Keep practising! *(20 marks)*
1. In the 1840s in America. *(2 marks)*
2. Women were not admitted to colleges to be trained as doctors. *(2 marks)*
3. *Possible places:* before "Elizabeth applied …"; before "The professors …" *(2 marks)*
4. a) women – adjective; b) ridiculous – adjective; c) several – adjective; d) unanimously – adverb. *(4 marks)*
5. Any three of these: was thought, were (not) allowed, was rejected, was admitted, was introduced, were encouraged. *(3 marks)*
6. positively, quietly, badly, politely. *(4 marks)*
7. Any two of these: At the time, Each time, until, when. *(2 marks)*

Take up the challenge! *(15 marks)*
1. Who – Dr Alexander Fleming; when – 1920s; where – London. *(3 marks)*
2. It is an adjective. *(1 mark)*
3. germs *(1 mark)*
4. He uses the time connective "His first step" at the beginning of the second paragraph to link with "wanted to find a way" in the first paragraph. *(2 marks)*
5. that could kill the germs; in which harmful bacteria were growing *(2 marks)*
6. Bold type is used to emphasise "was" and to show Fleming's determination. *(2 marks)*
7. They were both able to kill or prevent the growth of harmful bacteria. In other words, they had antibiotic qualities. *(2 marks)*
8. They prevent infection and can destroy harmful bacteria that have already entered a person's body. This enables people to stay alive and live longer. *(2 marks)*

EXTENSION ACTIVITIES

- Children could look at texts in other subject areas that tell of past events (e.g. history, science, music, art) and identify in them the characteristic language features of recount texts.
- Children could write an account of something interesting that happened at school recently. They could then compare versions, looking specifically at effective verbs and time connectives.

Giving instructions

FOCUS   To revise the form and language used in instructions: (6.3. S1)
Scottish 5–14: As pupils acquire experience across a wide variety of forms, the teacher will point out the positive effects of careful and imaginative layout and presentation

TEACHER INFORMATION

- Instructions and procedural texts outline what needs to be done to reach a particular objective. Typically, they begin by stating the objective. What follows is a step-by-step guide through the actions, using imperative sentences. Instructional texts are characterised by lists (of things needed and of the steps themselves), numbers, bullet points and sequencing connectives to make the order clearer.
- The emphasis for children, in revising the features of instructional texts, should be on clear, simple language and formats that make instructions easy to follow.

ANSWERS TO PUPIL'S BOOK

Try it out!   *(20 marks)*
Many of the answers will vary. Example answers are given.
1. Step 1: Look; Step 2: test; Step 3: Put; Step 4: Place, seen *(2.5 marks)*
2. Step 5: sign; Step 6; bait; Step 7: trap, house; Step 8: process *(2.5 marks)*
3. The word "humane" means "compassionate" or "inflicting little pain". *(1 mark)*
4. They could be put into a list with bullet points. *(2 marks)*
5. *Any four from:* First, Then, Next, When, Finally *(2 marks)*
6. Close your door after each inspection. *(2 marks)*
7. How to send an email *(2 marks)*
8. The second and third steps are in the wrong order. *(2 marks)*
9. The steps could be numbered to make the sequence clearer. *(2 marks)*
10. Close your email software program. *(2 marks)*

Keep practising!   *(20 marks)*
Some answers will vary. Example answers are given.
1. She wanted to know how to repair a leaking tap so that next time she could do the work herself and not have to pay a plumber. *(2 marks)*
2. How to repair a leaking tap *(2 marks)*
3. Step 10 is unnecessary because the idea is covered in Step 9. *(2 marks)*
4. Make sure you have a wrench and several different washers. *(2 marks)*
5. Put on a new washer, screw the tap on again and turn on the mains tap. *(2 marks)*
6. Steps 11 and 12 are conditional sentences. The conditional connectives are "If" (step 11) and "In the unlikely event" (step 12). *(4 marks)*
7. Step 2: *First* …; Step 3: *Then* …; Step 4: *Next* … *(6 marks)*

Take up the challenge!   *(20 marks)*
Open-ended. Award marks flexibly for clearly stated and formatted instructions.

EXTENSION ACTIVITIES

- Ask pupils to give oral directions/instructions for common situations (e.g. how to get from home to school, how to wash a car). Record the instructions. Then ask the children to put the instructions into a written format.

Writing reports

FOCUS To revise characteristic features of non-chronological report texts: (6.3. S1)
Scottish 5–14: As pupils acquire experience across a wide variety of forms, the
teacher will point out the positive effects of careful and imaginative layout and
presentation

TEACHER INFORMATION

- Report texts present information on a subject in such a way as to describe the
way things are in an objective, impersonal way. The writing is well-organised
and structured, though not always chronologically. Report texts often begin
with an idea of the subject matter and then move on to details. Often they end
with a brief summary. They are usually written in the present tense – conveying
continuing and timeless action.
- Some children have a tendency to revert to narrative writing in the middle of
report. The distinctive impersonal and objective tone of report writing needs a
great deal of practice. Fortunately, report writing links well to other subject
areas that can provide useful contexts.

ANSWERS TO PUPIL'S BOOK

Try it out!   *(20 marks)*
1. It presents a general idea of the subject matter. *(1 mark)*
2. They are arranged in order of size, starting with the smallest bird. *(1 marks)*
3. *Any 6 from:* hops, searches, dart, rush, attack, tear, eat, steal, swoop, pounce, fly off, glide *(3 marks)*
4. *Any 8 from:* nervous, perky, territorial, bold, quick-tempered, multi-coloured, arrogant, strutting, sly, deadly, unsuspecting *(4 marks)*
5. From time to time, large predators can be seen. *(1 mark)*
6. The colon introduces the various kinds of tits. *(1 mark)*
7. No colon is needed after "include". There is no break in the sentence. The birds that follow are the direct object of "include". *(1 mark)*
8. The dash forces the reader to pause briefly and realise that a change of some sort is coming. *(1 mark)*
9. "Deadly" is not an adverb. *(1 mark)*
10. The word is "territorial", i.e. they defend their own territory. *(1 mark)*
11. The subheading "Larger predators" could be placed before the final paragraph. *(1 mark)*
12. a) at the end of the third paragraph;
    b) at the beginning of the first paragraph;
    c) in brackets in the first sentence of "Big birds" section;
    d) after the last sentence;
    e) before the last sentence in the second paragraph;
    f) in the first paragraph;
    g) at the end of the second paragraph;
    h) within the first sentence of the second paragraph. *(4 marks)*

Keep practising!   *(20 marks)*
1. Alice is 11. She says her brother, who is 14, is three years older. *(2 marks)*
2. vaccuum – vacuum; completly – completely; marshal – martial; poplar – popular; there hands – their hands; truble – trouble *(3 marks)*
3. line 2: baby. To me; line 4: bin. There; line 7: her. At; line 15: homework. I *(2 marks)*

4. line 3: He eats; line 11: ever tries *(2 marks)*
5. It is a simile. It makes the description more vivid and concrete. *(2 marks)*
6. The letters "V. C." are short for "vacuum-cleaner" and indicate that Bill eats more than a normal person. *(1 mark)*
7. The past tense is used to describe an incident that happened in the past and that demonstrates one of Bill's good points. *(2 marks)*
8. *Open-ended. Award marks flexibly for thoughtful answers, for example:*
   Start with a description of his *physical appearance*: size, face, hair, clothes. Then give an account of his *character*, with examples of incidents that reveal his character. Describe some of his hobbies and interests and then, perhaps, his future ambitions. *(6 marks)*

Take up the challenge! *(20 marks)*
1. The first paragraph sets out what the report is about. *(2 marks)*
2. It has been created by converting part of the upstairs landing. *(1 mark)*
3. What follows the colon shows how the bedrooms were used. *(1 mark)*
4. Second paragraph: "Hey presto" – slang exclamation more appropriate to speech.
   Third paragraph use of the 2nd person, including an imperative sentence, which addresses the reader in a personal way. *(4 marks)*
5. *Open-ended. Examples are:* Where it is; How it was built; What it looks like; How I feel about it. *(4 marks)*
6. *Main clauses:* my room is warm and comfortable; There is a radiator behind the desk; We cannot afford to move to a bigger house.
   Subordinate clauses: Although it is small and very cramped; so I never feel chilly; so I just have to settle for my space on the landing *(6 marks)*
7. *Open-ended. Possible answer:* "Cage" refers to a place where someone or something is confined, like a wild animal. Mike's family are comparing him humorously to a wild animal. *(6 marks)*

EXTENSION ACTIVITIES

- Children can try writing brief report texts describing, say, an animal or an object. They could then read their report to an audience, deleting all specific references to the "thing". Others have to guess what the subject is.

- Children could be asked to research a given topic and to read a variety of report texts on that topic. They could then explore and compare those texts, identifying the characteristic features. Hopefully, there will be examples of texts that are not "pure" reports, leading to a discussion about hybrid texts that are a mix of genres.

- Give each child a copy of PCM15 "School report" (page 70) to complete.

unit 20 Persuasive writing

FOCUS   To investigate and revise the characteristic features of persuasive writing: (6.3. S1)
Scottish 5–14: Sentence structures can be discussed in terms of how they create
meaning, mood and atmosphere

TEACHER INFORMATION

- Persuasive writing attempts to convince the reader to accept the writer's point of view. Persuasive texts can include a wide variety of formats from tinned food labels and classified ads to letters and political manifestos. The lines between persuasive writing and discursive writing are often blurred, but persuasive texts normally present one viewpoint only, while discursive texts set out both (or all) sides of an issue.

- The language and techniques used by the "persuader" depend very much on the intended "market" or audience. They can be blatant and highly visual; or they can be very subtle and almost subliminal. Encourage children to think carefully about their intended audience when writing persuasively, and to use words and techniques appropriately.

ANSWERS TO PUPIL'S BOOK

Try it out!   *(20 marks)*

1. Advertisement B looks more attractive. The reasons for this include: the use of bold type; the inclusion of a picture; the less crowded layout. *(3 marks)*
2. a) The total prices are the same. *(1 mark)*
   b) Omission of the delivery charge makes the price seem lower, and this makes the reader think he is getting a better bargain. *(1 mark)*
3. a) cancelled; recession *(1 mark)*
   b) *Any two of these:* super, free, discount, latest, deluxe, guarantee *(1 mark)*
4. *Buy, get* in advertisement B. *(2 marks)*
5. There is probably an order form in the bottom half. *(2 marks)*
6. a) No; b) Yes; c) Yes (probably); d) Yes; e) No. *(5 marks)*
7. *Open-ended.* Most children will opt for advertisement B because it is presented more persuasively, offers a free 14-day trial and 12-month guarantee, and outlines more technical features. However, some children may claim that the advertisement A offer, on close reading, is quite similar – perhaps they prefer a "no-nonsense" presentation. *(4 marks)*

Keep practising!   *(20 marks)*

1. *Answers will vary. Examples are:* a) magnificent, snap up; b) jumbo jumble (alliteration), fat wallets (imagery); c) volunteer, come; d) therefore, so; e) **please** (bold); BARGAINS (capital letters). *(5 marks)*
2. a) The idea of getting a bargain might be attractive. *(1 mark)*
   b) "Jumbo" is used cleverly to alliterate with "jumble" and implies that the bargains will be big ones. *(1 mark)*
3. magnificent, opportunity, grateful, secretary, customers, proceeds *(3 marks)*
4. At the end of the first paragraph: a colon because what follows lists the "ways"; at the end of point 3: exclamation mark to show the humour of what precedes it. *(4 marks)*
5. Each of the three numbered points begins with an imperative verb in capital letters. They pick out the three most important points of the letter: bring, volunteer, come. *(2 marks)*
6. It may make them more willing to volunteer to help because they will get first pick of the jumble. *(1 mark)*
7. *Answers will vary. Examples are:* Yes, it is effective because it grabs the reader's attention with well-chosen words and phrases, and uses humour and presentational devices. **Or** No, it is not

effective because the message gets lost in the overuse of presentational devices. *(3 marks)*

Take up the challenge! *(20 marks)*

1. "For sale" could be omitted because all ads in this section of the paper will be "for sale" ones. *(2 marks)*
2. buyer (A); men's, rallies (C); tyres (D) *(2 marks)*
3. The price is missing from A. *(1 mark)*
4. *Any three of these:* great value; superb condition; ideal; 1st class; top quality; bargain. *(3 marks)*
5. "Recently repaired" might have a negative effect, indicating that the bike has been damaged. *(2 marks)*
6. It's probably not a good idea. People will be looking in the classified ads for a specific item. Therefore, the item should come first. *(2 marks)*
7. "Ono" means "or nearest offer". *(1 mark)*
8. David has written "Very little use" instead of "Used very little". Some buyers might think that the bicycle really is of very little use. *(2 marks)*
9. D contains 23 words, three words must be deleted: possibly all of "Very little use", or "on", "any day". *(2 marks)*
10. Open-ended. *(3 marks)*

EXTENSION ACTIVITIES

- Pupils can investigate advertisements, newspaper editorials and letters to the editor, and other persuasive texts in which the choice of individual words (and perhaps the layout) are important.
- Record a television programme in which panellists are required to give their opinions on current affairs or other issues. Children can listen to it, and collect and study examples of effective persuasive techniques.

unit 21

Writing discussion texts

FOCUS   To investigate and revise the characteristic features of discussion texts: (6.3. S1)
Scottish 5–14: Purpose and audience will feature regularly when pupils consider
what they plan to write or what they have written

TEACHER INFORMATION

- Although the focus here has to be largely on the language involved, the
  following points also merit consideration – and are of value beyond the
  classroom. In dealing with an argumentative topic:
  - Consider what your task is. Do you have to discuss it, prove that it is true or
    reject it?
  - Consider both sides in an objective way.
  - Arrange your points in a logical order, perhaps in order of importance.
  - Don't exaggerate. Don't lie. Don't be abusive.
  - Understand the difference between facts and opinions.
  - Avoid dogmatic statements as far as possible.
  - Give evidence or supporting material.

ANSWERS TO PUPIL'S BOOK

Try it out!   *(20 marks)*
Answers may vary. Examples are:
1. a) *modal verbs* – may be, should think, may not become, should use; b) *adjectives that show
   judgement* – dangerous, useful, false, unproven; c) *connectives that indicate opposition* – whether …
   or not, on the other hand, however. *(3 marks)*
2. No, we cannot use "are" instead of "may be" because scientists are not yet certain whether
   mobile phones are a hazard or not. *(2 marks)*
3. No, we cannot safely use "must". There is inadequate scientific evidence to justify "must".
   (2 marks)
4. weather – whether; noticable – noticeable; precortion – precaution; sauce – source; exposer –
   exposure; recieving – receiving *(3 marks)*
5. first paragraph: years later when it; second paragraph: known. Parents *(2 marks)*
6. may, to *(2 marks)*
7. It means "the other way round", i.e. children can keep in touch with their parents. *(1 mark)*
8. c) against trouble *(1 mark)*
9. c) mobile phones *(1 mark)*
10. 200 (20%) *(1 mark)*
11. Children do not have to hold the mobile phone up to their head when they are texting.
    (2 marks)

Keep practising!   *(20 marks)*
1. because *(1 mark)*
2. We could use a semicolon or a dash. *(2 marks)*
3. She is warning of a change in her reasoning or attitude. *(2 marks)*
4. A cyclist would pay £18, i.e. 10% of £180. *(2 marks)*
5. Her last sentence is not accurate. Cyclists **do** take up space on roads and contribute to the wear
   and tear on roads. *(2 marks)*
6. He could use "For a start" or "Firstly". *(1 mark)*
7. defenitely – definitely; to poor – too poor; goverment – government; exaust – exhaust
   (4 marks)
8. He is giving another reason for disagreeing with a proposal to make cyclists pay a licence fee.
   (2 marks)

9. In addition *(1 mark)*
10. *Answers will vary. Example:* I agree with Danny. Many cyclists are poor. Some people cycle to improve their health. Cyclists do not cause pollution of the air and should be encouraged. *(3 marks)*

Take up the challenge! *(20 marks)*
Exercise: is, will, may, are, will
Television: most, all, most, none, a few
Cycling helmets: often, seldom, often, always, never
Traffic accidents: however, in spite of, in addition, in spite of, on the contrary.

EXTENSION ACTIVITIES

- Let pupils debate/discuss some of the issues presented in the Pupil's Book, while other pupils comment on the use of appropriate language and balance.
- Give pupils a single sentence and ask them to suggest a second sentence (supporting or opposing), using different links at the start of the second sentence – for example:
  - All homework should be abolished.
  - Cats make better pets than dogs.
- Pupils could watch some interviews or debates on television, and discuss how the characteristic features of discussion are evident – or not, as the case may be!

Investigating English expressions

FOCUS   To investigate the English language to find out how it works: (6.3. S2)
Scottish 5–14: Examining the relationships of words and meanings

TEACHER INFORMATION

- The underlying aim of this unit is to encourage pupils to do their own research into how the language works, how it has changed and how it is still changing. The scope of the unit is almost limitless. An additional obvious target for investigation is the dialect prevalent in the local area.

ANSWERS TO PUPIL'S BOOK

Try it out!   *(10 marks)*
1. (11) is opposite in meaning to (1).
2. (9) is similar in meaning to (5).
3. (6) is somewhat similar to (14).
4. (2) is opposite in meaning to (16).
5. (4), (7) and (10) mean roughly the same as "Make the most of your opportunities".
6. (6) and (14) mean roughly "Stay out of trouble".
7. (15) is both similar and opposite to (3). Both proverbs refer to large groups of people (who think alike), but (3) refers to wise men while (15) refers to fools.
8. She could say, "Half a loaf is better than none" or, "A bird in the hand is worth two in the bush".
9. They said, "Too many cooks spoil the broth."
10. If you wake a dog up, it may bite you, so it is best to let it stay asleep. Similarly if you disturb a situation that is currently peaceful, you may instigate trouble.

Keep practising!   *(10 marks)*
1–12 (8 marks – 0.5 mark for each correct answer)
1. m; 2. k; 3. c; 4. f; 5. p; 6. e; 7. a; 8. o; 9. b, n; 10. j, l; 11. h, d; 12. i, g.
13. Answers will vary depending on which two idioms the children choose. *(2 marks)*

Take up the challenge!   *(10 marks)*
Answers will vary. Examples are:
1. Stop doing that. You're annoying me.
2. I do not understand that.
3. Doing homework is hard and dull.
4. This place is messy and unpleasant. It also has a bad smell.
5. I can't go because I haven't got any money.
6. Turn off the television and stop being lazy and inactive.
7. She's just trying to be like a pop-star and is trying to start her career quickly.
8. Don't spend time with them. They are troublesome.
9. Don't be so bad-tempered. Be calm.
10. Did you really spend all that money on this car, which is in such bad condition?

EXTENSION ACTIVITIES

- Children could investigate local dialect, the language of a soap opera, advertising or computers, puns (intended or not), etc.
- Give each child a copy of PCM16 "Cockney rhyming slang" (page 71) to complete.

Assessment 3

ANSWERS TO PUPIL'S BOOK

Using the right verb form *(6 marks – 0.5 mark for each correct answer)*

1. heard
2. coming
3. discovered
4. was playing
5. was collecting, collected
6. passed
7. was
8. went
9. asked
10. could be making, could make
11. would have been deceiving, would have deceived
12. sing

Parts of speech *(4 marks – 0.5 mark for each correct answer)*

1. Hey!
2. noun
3. preposition
4. relative pronoun
5. solemnly
6. There are four verbs: was playing; sang; was collecting; passed
7. popular, busy, One
8. "They" refers to the man and his two animals.

Using "a" and "an" *(5 marks – 0.5 mark for each correct answer)*

1. a
2. a
3. a
4. an, a
5. an, an
6. an
7. a, an

Using capital letters *(10 marks – 2 marks for each sentence with correct capital letters)*

1. January, February, North (Africa)
2. English, Mrs (Baker)
3. South Wales, Bristol
4. Monday, May
5. Expectations, Charles Dickens, Victorian

Joining sentences *(5 marks)*
Alternatives are possible.

1. Although Ruby liked the red dress, she decided not to buy it because it was too expensive.
2. Where have you put the apples you bought at the farmers' market yesterday?
3. That's the house where my new friend from India lives.
4. The woman whose car was damaged was very angry because the other motorist refused to pay for the damage, claiming that it was not his fault.
5. The factory in which my father used to work has closed down, so he has changed his job.
   My father has changed his job because the factory where he used to work has closed down.

Prepositions *(10 marks – 0.5 mark for each correct answer)*

1. from
2. for
3. down
4. into
5. near
6. with
7. across
8. to
9. to
10. behind
11. up/down
12. by
13. under
14. of
15. about
16. with
17. of
18. in
19. of
20. in

Say it another way *(5 marks – 0.5 mark for each correct sentence)*

1. There is no need for you to wash the dishes.
   You need not wash the dishes.
2. Many trees were blown down by a hurricane last night.
3. Both of the robbers will soon be caught by the police.
4. It was unwise of Mary to argue with Miss Evans about such a trivial point.
5. The plumber explained to us how best to repair the tap.
6. It is time the game started.
7. It took me half an hour to solve the problem.
8. The woman accused the man of having tried (of trying) to snatch her bag.

9. An explorer's life can be full of excitement and danger.

10. Mary wondered how the woman had managed to open the door.

Reported (indirect) speech *(5 marks – 0.5 mark for each correct sentence)*

1. Matthew told me on the phone that he might come and see me the next day.
2. The two girls told Ashra that they would wait for her at the station. They told her to try not to be late.
3. A tourist asked my brother if he could (please) tell him the way to the airport.
4. My mother asked me if I had finished my homework yet.
5. Davina told me that she was going into town and asked me if I wanted to go with her.
6. I asked Daljit if anybody had been hurt in the fire.
7. Paul asked his mother if she had seen his purple shirt.
8. The stranger asked us if the last bus had gone already. He wanted to know the nearest place where he could get a taxi.
9. Tony asked his sister if he could borrow her bicycle on the following Saturday. He promised that he would return it on the following Sunday morning.
10. Tom asked Susan whether she still lived in Trenton Road or whether she had already moved to Stanton.

Punctuation *(15 marks)*

Answers will vary. Award marks flexibly for sensible and accurate punctuation. An example is:

We entered the ruins of the old house cautiously. It was dark and gloomy inside. The windows, which were boarded up, kept the light and air out, creating damp and musty air inside. We moved slowly along the corridor, not knowing what to expect next. When we reached the first room, the door was closed.

"Be careful!" I warned. "We don't know what we might find inside."

Disregarding my warning, Mike opened the door and ventured forth. The rest of us crept loyally in behind him, flashing our torches from side to side. Relief flooded over us; there was nobody in the room and no obvious signs that the room had been inhabited recently.

We were just starting to relax a bit when we heard the sound: a groan – or maybe it was a sigh. "It's coming from over there," I whispered fearfully, pointing to what looked like a pile of rags in the far corner. We approached the pile of rags nervously. Who or what might be hiding there? Uncertain what to do next, Mike prodded the rags gingerly with his stick, half expecting something large and wild to leap out of them. Again we heard the sound – definitely a groan. The hair on the back of my neck stuck out like the spines on a hedgehog. We all shone our torches on the rags and watched as Mike pulled some of them away. Then we gasped when the head and face (if that's what we could call it) of a tiny weird creature peered up at us, dazzled by the light from our torches.

Choose the word *(10 marks – 1 mark for each correct answer)*

1. if, gone
2. it's, have played
3. until, came
4. who, their
5. Maybe, by

Answers to Workbook

Unit 1: Word classes

Work it out *(10 marks)*
Accept suitable alternative answers.

1. Rome	5. everyone/everybody	9. skilfully
2. foolish/stupid	6. February	10. lengthen
3. flock	7. often/frequently	
4. shiver	8. but	

Which word? *(10 marks)*

1. anything	3. is	5. effect	7. me	9. take
2. waiting	4. are	6. impatient	8. from	10. Paul's

Classify it *(10 marks – 0.5 mark for each correctly placed word)*
Nouns: couple, Squeers, cruelty
Pronouns: that, he, who
Verbs: was, faded, crowded
Adjectives: rickety, cut, every, stooping
Adverbs: around, hardly
Prepositions: for, with
Conjunctions: but, whether, and

Unit 2: Using standard English

Does it agree? *(14 marks)*
In some cases, the subject (S) can be longer than the one given below.

1. S: How much of the information … is	8. S: audience … is
2. S: reward … has	9. S: Everybody … wants
3. S: driver … was	10. S: all this rubbish … has
4. S: mud … Is	11. S: the poor … are
5. S: The number of flights … has	12. S: standard … is
6. S: a number of reasons … are	13. S: a third … are
7. S: traffic … has	14. S: majority of the pupils … do

Choose the right word *(8 marks)*

1. or	3. it	5. worse	7. equipment
2. nor	4. any	6. and I, them	8. may be

Make it formal *(8 marks)*

1. bad	5. anyone/anybody
2. in difficulties	6. is very obvious
3. children	7. becoming more popular
4. anything	8. How has it happened that/Why is it that

Unit 3: Active and passive verbs 1

A dangerous job *(12 marks)*

1. is grown	4. is made	7. is emptied	10. is squeezed
2. are attacked	5. is fastened	8. is taken	11. are hung
3. are sometimes mistaken	6. is used	9. are added	12. are tied

A gas leak *(10 marks)*

1. has been wrecked	5. has been brought	9. have been evacuated
2. Has … been injured	6. has been informed	10. have been moved
3. have been hurt	7. has been hurled	
4. have been taken	8. have been broken	

In trouble *(8 marks)*

1. will be charged
2. will be asked
3. will be told
4. will be given
5. will be invited
6. will be informed
7. will be banned
8. will be fined

Unit 4: Connectives

Types of connectives *(10 marks)*
Addition: (3) and then; (7) or; (8) Moreover
Time: (2) when; (4) Following
Cause/effect: (5) if; (6) because
Opposition: (1) although; (9) but; (10) Despite

Connective starters *(10 marks)*
Open-ended. Accept all suitable answers. Examples are:

1. we can get a taxi
2. you'll be sorry later
3. it was much too heavy
4. the snow soon melted
5. we decided to go for a walk
6. she has a cat and a dog
7. pay for them
8. I was late for school
9. the heavy rain
10. my brother never eats it

Choosing connectives *(10 marks)*

1. Alternatively
2. Despite
3. meantime
4. Furthermore
5. Consequently
6. For example
7. contrary
8. Nevertheless
9. instead of
10. so that

Unit 5: Forming complex sentences 1

Completing sentences *(10 marks)*
Open-ended. Accept all suitable answers. Examples are:
1. *where* we can read and borrow books.
2. *where* the seven dwarfs lived with Snow White.
3. *when* you come to bed.
4. *when* they have toothache or need to have their teeth checked.
5. *if* you water them regularly.
6. *if* he appears to be driving too fast or recklessly.
7. *so* she had to stay at home.
8. *so* he turned the volume up.
9. *provided that* you're back here before it gets dark.
10. *provided that* you return it before Saturday afternoon

What and where? *(10 marks)*
Open-ended. Accept all suitable answers. Examples are:
1. discussing their neighbour on a bus.
2. peering into one of the cars at the side of the road.
3. pulling their net out of the sea.
4. trying to get a kite down from a tree.
5. searching for food in the garden.
6. learning to ski on a slope in Scotland.
7. straying away from their mothers about twenty metres from the gate.
8. moving about in the living-room.
9. working hard in his front garden.
10. shouting "Help!" about forty metres from the shore.

Punctuating complex sentences *(10 marks)*

1. Yesterday, in broad daylight, the police caught two men trying to rob a bank.
2. The frightened rabbit stayed absolutely still, hoping that the fox had not seen it.
3. My father, the manager of the store, starts work before 8 a.m.
4. Last night the temperature in most Welsh towns was above freezing-point. In Aberystwyth, however, it was minus four degrees.
5. Did you enjoy yourself at the party last Saturday, Kate?
6. Although the concert lasted for over two hours, the audience was captivated by the soloist, who was only ten.
7. Not having seen her cousin for several years, Sue was surprised to see how tall he was.
8. Birmingham is a very large city. In fact, it is one of the largest in the United Kingdom.
9. When the phone rang, Peter hurried to answer it, hoping that it was his friend.
10. Leaping over the wall, the frightened animal, disappeared into the woods.

Unit 6: Punctuation

Using commas *(10 marks)*

1. The home of the Duke of Devonshire has 173 rooms, and houses more than 60 types of clocks.
2. Paul, go and find Mary, please.
3. Worms are probably the most common bait for fish. If you expect to catch fish, therefore, you must be prepared to handle worms.
4. "Ugh! I'm not going to touch a worm," Katie said.
5. One of our neighbours, Mrs Collins, is a very experienced nurse.
6. Even if I were a billionaire, I would not want to live alone in a huge, isolated house.
7. Very few people read poetry books in their leisure time. Many modern pop songs, however, contain their own type of poetry and are very popular.
8. When tadpoles get older, their tails get shorter, their legs get longer and they gradually develop into very small frogs.
9. Pauline Taylor, whose father is a maths teacher, is always top of the class in maths, not surprisingly.
10. If you're ready, it's time for us to leave for the airport, Grandad.

Using speech marks *(10 marks)*

NB: If children have used single speech marks, then speech marks within them should be double. If they have used double speech marks, then speech marks within them should be single.

1. My friend said to me, "Would you mind checking this letter for me, please?"
2. I told her, "You've left an 'r' out of 'preferred'."
3. Miss Lee told me, "You should have written 'chose' and not 'choose'."
4. I heard Paul shout out, "Wait for me, Mike!" so we waited for him.
5. "If you've finished your homework," my mother said, "you can watch the cartoons on TV."
6. When the performance ended, the audience rose to their feet and shouted, "Bravo!"
7. Clamouring up the treacherous rocks, the mountain rescuer cried, "Hold on!"
8. "Can I follow you?" asked Grace. "I don't know the way. Besides, it's dark."
9. The wizard, whose wand was misbehaving, shook his finger and said, "Abracadabra!"
10. Louise rubbed her eyes, yawned and mumbled, "What's the matter?"

More punctuation practice *(10 marks)*

1. It's the end of March tomorrow. Remember to put your clocks on an hour.
2. Remember what people say in America: "Spring forward; Fall back."
   or "Spring, forward. Fall, back."
3. In sentence 2, "fall" means "autumn".
4. There are 24 children in our class: 14 boys and 10 girls.
5. I think that jacket is a real bargain, don't you, Mary?
6. That was my first visit to a zoo. I thought it was very interesting.
7. "Come in. Sit down. Would you like a soft drink?" *(The speech marks can be omitted.)*
8. Some girls like to play netball or rounders; other prefer hockey.

9. The speaker promised the people many things: more jobs, higher pay, longer holidays and lower taxes.

10. Don't forget the saying: "Nothing ventured, nothing gained."

Unit 8: Active and passive verbs 2

Look to the future *(10 marks)*

1. will be closed
2. will be completed
3. will be reopened
4. will be diverted
5. will be put
6. will be held
7. will be cancelled
8. will be invited
9. will be told
10. will be postponed

Will, may or must? *(10 marks)*
Alternatives are possible in some cases.

1. must
2. may, may
3. may, may/will/must, will/may
4. must, must
5. will, may/will

Active to passive *(10 marks)*

1. Mr Jackson's car was stolen during the night.
2. Before the dentist drilled my tooth, I was given an injection.
3. That old factory was pulled down last week.
4. Two trees were blown down last night.
5. Mrs Sharpe has just been taken to hospital.
6. Our rubbish is collected every Friday.
7. A lot of apples are grown in this part of the country.
8. Sometimes swimmers are attacked not far from the beach.
9. The new school will be opened tomorrow.
10. Our school will be redecorated during the holidays.

Unit 9: Official language

What do they mean? *(10 marks)*

1. we have very considerable pleasure
2. requesting the pleasure of your company
3. sumptuous festive social gathering
4. young attractive females and boisterous males
5. anniversary of her blessed nativity
6. be informed
7. ancestral place of residence
8. drawing to a close
9. would greatly appreciate
10. all concerned

In translation *(10 marks)*
Award marks flexibly for correctly translating and communicating the main points, for example:
Mary has sent me an amusing, formal invitation to her eleventh birthday party. It will be at her home on the twenty-fifth of April from 4–8 p.m. She doesn't want any presents. I have to let her know if I'm coming by the twenty-first of April.

Keep it simple *(10 marks)*

1. write to him
2. your full name
3. If
4. because
5. guardian
6. ill/sick
7. alleged robber
8. kill/destroy/exterminate
9. investigated/considered
10. the decision

Unit 10: Forming complex sentences 2

Adding connectives *(10 marks)*

1. before, after
2. If, provided
3. so, although
4. so that, when
5. while, despite

Punctuating complex sentences *(10 marks – 2 marks for each correct sentence)*

1. We expected Tom's friend to come at 5 p.m. However, he didn't arrive until 5.30.
   (We can use p.m. or pm.)
2. In the middle of lunch, a boy rushed into the canteen(,) shouting "Fire! Fire!"
3. I put my books away and turned off the light. Then I went to bed.
4. When the phone rang, Maya picked it up, expecting to hear her friend's voice.
5. The answer Peter gave, although partially right, was not the right one. *(Dashes or brackets could also be used instead of the commas.)*

Joining sentences *(10 marks – 2.5 marks for each correct sentence)*
Alternatives are possible.

1. When the rain stopped, we played in the garden although the grass was still wet and we were quite chilly.
2. The girl who won lots of money and gave half of it to charity is Janet's cousin.
3. This is the beautiful ring that my aunt gave me when I was ten.
4. Although Uncle George is over fifty, he completed the marathon and raised lots of money for charity.

Unit 11: Making notes

NB: The following answers are only notes; they are not the messages that would be based on the notes. Answers will vary. Award marks flexibly for appropriate selection of information and note-making style. Examples are:

Babysitting *(10 marks)*

1. Peter Brown – can't come 10 am tomor – pl phone sec 099-438 tomor – make new appt – Thur or Fri a.m. fine.
2. Glunk Glass 25% off 1 week, 2 wind +. Can phone Andrew Brown furth det 047-738.

Customer services *(10 marks)*

1. Ivy Trott – no Milky Way Mousse in stock. Why not? Wants some.
2. (Name not given) 2 x bad tomatoes 6-pack – will check for improve. Expects refund.

Local newspaper reporter *(10 marks)*

1. past week, 6 cars vand in Leo's car pk 10 pm – 6 am. Informant has names and addr of 2 suspects.
2. suspic acts 39 Lufton Road – empty 6 mos, now people, goods lorries. Stolen goods? Rel burgls in area?

Unit 12: Writing a summary

One-word summaries *(10 marks)*

1. reservoir	3. tunnel	5. nurse	7. chewing	9. arrested
2. shuffling	4. bank	6. rain	8. impatient	10. skilfully

Headlines *(10 marks – 2 marks for each headline)*
We have to bear in mind that headlines do not usually include long words because of the lack of space and the need to create maximum effect.
1. House down shaft hole *("Hole" is redundant but is added for the benefit of readers who do not know what a shaft is!)*
2. "Panther" seen near Taunton *("Panther" is in inverted commas because it is a quotation and we cannot be sure that the animal really WAS a panther.)*
3. 500 not out!
4. "Delay killed girl" – parents' rage
5. Deadly spider found in grapes

What can you remember? *(10 marks – 2.5 marks for each sentence)*
Open-ended. Award 1 mark for keeping to the 20-word limit and 1 mark for a successful summary.

Unit 13: Editing

Using more effective words *(10 marks – 0.5 mark for each suitable answer)*
Answers will vary. Examples are:
1. came: rushed, dashed, hurried
2. said to: screamed at, shouted at
   loudly: madly, angrily, furiously
3. looked: glared, stared
   indicated: warned us, proved
4. moved: shuffled, limped, dragged himself
5. nice: attractive, beautiful, stunning
6. pulled apart: devastated, ripped in two
7. moved: limped, hobbled
   asking: begging, beseeching

Correcting errors *(10 marks – 0.5 mark for each correction)*
1. course; have/having; several
2. some pupils; obtain their
3. separate; lunch. The; earlier than; older pupils
4. food from; carefully. They are
5. questionnaire; food. We; from it; Appendix
6. that/which the pupils; too crowded; each table. This

Using headings *(10 marks)*
Answers will vary. Examples are:
1. Food; Canteen staff; Furniture; Scheduling; Pupils
2. Transport and cost; Date, times, parents; Food and drink; Entertainment; Weather

Unit 14: Conditional sentences

What happens? *(10 marks – 2 marks for each sentence)*
Answers will vary. Examples are:
1. … it gradually melts.
2. … the referee will probably show him a red card and send him off.
3. … they will set traps to catch the mice.
4. … we will probably see a rainbow.
5. … I'll get out of bed and go and have a drink.

What will probably happen? *(5 marks – 0.5 mark for each correct answer)*

1. plays, may start
2. will be postponed, will be held
3. eat, will put
4. will probably collapse, may break
5. will be flooded, may be forced

Giving advice *(10 marks – 2 marks for each suitable answer)*

1. If I were you, I'd go to bed earlier.
2. If I were you, I wouldn't drink it.
3. If I were you, I'd give them to a charity shop to sell.
4. If I were you, I'd avoid the ferry in case the weather is bad, and the train because I hear there might an industrial strike.
5. If I were you, I'd talk to the headteacher after school when other pupils have gone.

Other ways of showing a condition *(5 marks)*

1. You can go to Tom's house provided that you're back here by 8.00 p.m.
2. You can borrow my bike provided that you return it on Saturday.
3. Tom can stay with us for the weekend as long as his parents agree.
4. I'll help you as long as you don't argue all the time.
5. We can have a picnic on Saturday on condition that the weather is fine then.

Unit 16: Narrative writing

Zangram: **extract 1** *(10 marks)*

1. exhausted *(1 mark)*
2. She said, "We won't be down until noon." *(1 mark)*
3. "That's a" is missing; it is not essential in this type of direct, authentic speech. *(2 marks)*
4. a) soundly – quietly, deeply; b) contentedly – happily, noisily; c) silently – soundlessly, eerily; d) deeply – very, extremely *(4 marks)*
5. a) It tells us that the dogs were curious about what was going on.
   b) The cat was resentful because it was caught and failed to escape. *(2 marks)*

Zangram: **extract 2** *(10 marks)*

1. They were tested and examined for several days. *(2 marks)*
2. In the second paragraph, there is change of place – from inside the dome to outside it.
   In the third paragraph, direct speech starts a new paragraph.
   In the fourth paragraph, the narrative resumes after the direct speech. *(3 marks)*
3. The phrase "Outside the dome" creates a linked contrast to the phrase "in a huge dome". *(2 marks)*
4. It refers to what was happening outside the dome. *(1 mark)*
5. He uses a very short, simple sentence that changes the pace of the story. *(2 marks)*

Zangram: **extract 3** *(10 marks)*

1. They all end with a note of suspense. What is going to happen next? *(2 marks)*
2. The author uses … (ellipsis) to show that the speech was interrupted. *(1 mark)*
3. Uses of capital letters: for the name of a person or place (Tony Logan, Stonehenge); for the name of a month (July, August); for an abbreviation (Mrs); to start a new sentence; and to start direct speech. *(5 marks)*
4. *Open-ended. (2 marks)*

Unit 17: Describing past events

Time connectives *(10 marks)*

1. At the start of the game
2. within the first ten minutes
3. Ten minutes later
4. for the rest of the first half

5. At half-time
6. during the half-time break
7. Shortly afterwards
8. immediately
9. Ten minutes from the end
10. right up to the final whistle.

Exploring language *(20 marks)*
1. a) *Answers will vary. Examples are:* her, remote, rural, tasty, tiny, brown, clean, hot, hungry, thin *(5 marks)*
   b) *Answers will vary. Examples are:* rural – urban; tasty – tasteless; tiny – huge; clean – dirty; hot – cold; thin – thick *(3 marks)*
2. Answers will vary. Examples are: went, goes, will go; cooked, cooks, will cook; studied, studies, will study. *(3 marks)*
3. so *(1 mark)*
4. She did not want to upset her grandfather. *(1 mark)*
5. make a comparison. *(1 mark)*
6. a) *Answers will vary. Examples are:* very, thoughtfully, hesitantly, quickly, firmly, absolutely, immediately, furiously, angrily, quietly *(3 marks)*
   b) *Answers will vary. Examples are:* very – slightly; hesitantly – confidently; quickly – slowly; quietly – noisily *(2 marks)*
7. She meant that she had been deceived or tricked. *(1 mark)*

Unit 18: Giving instructions

Checklist *(15 marks)*
Some answers may vary. Example answers are given.
1. They are adverbs. *(2 marks)*
2. Check if front and rear lights are working. *(2 marks)*
3. He could sit on the saddle and try it out. *(2 marks)*
4. (Step 3) battery; (Step 5) comfortable; (Step 6) loose; (Step 9) axles. *(4 marks)*
5. Check that the bell is fastened firmly and working properly. *(2 marks)*
6. Steps 8 and 10 could be combined as they both deal with the tyres. *(2 marks)*
7. It is to be able to lock up the bicycle and deter thieves. *(1 mark)*

Defrosting a freezer *(15 marks)*
Answers will vary. Example answer might be:
1. Get some old towels and a pail or saucepan.
2. Turn off the electricity and empty the freezer. Put any packets in the fridge.
3. Put a towel on the floor at the front of the freezer.
4. Put some towels inside the freezer to absorb water.
5. Leave the door of the freezer open.
6. Put a bowl of hot water in the freezer if you are in a hurry.
7. When the ice has melted, take out the wet towels and wring them out.
8. Clean and dry the freezer.
9. Put the packets back in the freezer.
10. Turn the freezer back on.

Unit 19: Writing reports

The breakfast report *(10 marks)*
1. *Open-ended. Possible answer:* When we eat; Where we eat; What we eat *(3 marks)*
2. *Open-ended. Possible answer:* "Sitting-down" breakfast; "Standing-up" breakfast; "On-the-move" breakfast *(3 marks)*
3. classified – adjective; leisurely – adjective; c) usually – adverb; d) verb (4 marks)

The rodent report *(10 marks)*

1. a) were brought *(1 mark)*
   b) The emphasis here is on squirrels and not on the people who brought them to Britain. *(1 mark)*
2. What they eat *(2 marks)*
3. so; However; Therefore; since; *(2 marks)*
4. excaped – escaped; presents – presence; naturaly – naturally; poeple's – people's *(2 marks)*
5. *Main clause:* In some towns, squirrels in parks are so tame
   Subordinate clause: that they will take peanuts, if offered, from people's hands *(2 marks)*

Write a worm report *(10 marks)*

Open-ended. Award marks flexibly for appropriate headings; notes allocated to appropriate headings, and sentences that are in the present tense and an impersonal style. Suggested headings might be: What worms look like; Where worms live; What worms eat; How worms help us.

Unit 20: Persuasive writing

Email scam *(10 marks)*

1. immediate cancellation *(1 mark)*
2. " … bank had a failure … " because it happened yesterday. *(2 marks)*
3. a) software. This; b) data. This is *(2 marks)*
4. a) to your – of your; b) from fraud – delete "from"; c) connect with – connect to; d) answer to – omit "to". *(2 marks)*
5. lost – loss; Acount – Account *(2 marks)*
6. He is trying to coerce the receiver into supplying details of his bank account. *(1 mark)*

An advertisement *(10 marks)*

1. hep, cool *(1 mark)*
2. Alliteration is used (hep, handy, helpful). *(1 mark)*
3. Capital letters are used to emphasise the word and make it more prominent. *(1 mark)*
4. The writer wants to simulate speech, making the advertisement seem informal and personal *(2 marks)*
5. He uses "nifty" because he thinks that it is a word that younger readers use and will readily understand and relate to. It also establishes a bond with the readers. *(1 mark)*
6. The pictures are used to show the reader that popular celebrities (both male and female) have bought the watch and that it's a trendy thing to have. *(2 marks)*
7. Press the button – imperative; It tells you – Simple Present. *(1 mark)*
8. She thinks that the idea of moving up a grade or class has more appeal than merely staying at your existing level. The advertisement may then appeal to people who feel left behind or inferior. *(1 mark)*

Getting involved *(10 marks)*

1. They want to show why action is needed to make Bridge Street safer. *(1 mark)*
2. horrific, beg – the words are used to appeal to the councillors' emotions and persuade them to take action. *(2 marks)*
3. past, accidents, pedestrian, erect, signs, allowed *(3 marks)*
4. a) school. Each; b) Street. Finally we *(1 mark)*
5. was knocked down *(1 mark)*
6. First of all, Secondly, Thirdly, Finally *(1 mark)*
7. *Answers will vary. Example:* The recommendations could be set out as bulleted or numbered text so that it is clear that there are four separate suggestions. *(1 mark)*

Unit 21: Writing discussion texts

Television: points of view *(10 marks)*
1. The writer can replace "most" with "some" each time. *(1 mark)*
2. line 1: to – on; line 3: to – for/by *(2 marks)*
3. The subject is "Violence", so "are" should be changed to "is". *(1 mark)*
4. The writer has used a double negative. The second main clause should read: *… and do not cause any harm or offence. (1 mark)*
5. documentries – documentaries; intresting – interesting; affect – effect; principals – principles; chose – choose; breathe – breath *(3 marks)*
6. *Open-ended. Example:* The writer's discussion is balanced because it presents points supporting both sides of the argument, and a non-partisan conclusion. *(2 marks)*

Maths – or no maths? *(10 marks)*
1. lifes – life or lives; calculaters – calculators; compulsery – compulsory; waist – waste *(2 marks)*
2. agree with; difficult for *(1 mark)*
3. The writer could use "dishonest people" instead of "crooks", and "bored" instead of "fed up". *(1 mark)*
4. *Answers will vary. Example:* The writer gives two arguments for not studying maths (although they are not in the same paragraph): 1) computers and calculators can do the job for us; 2) algebra and geometry are too difficult making children hate the subject and misbehave. The writer also gives two arguments *for* studying maths (although the first is really part of the second: 1) we need to know maths so we are not taken advantage of by dishonest people; 2) we need maths when we buy or sell things. *(4 marks)*
5. *Open-ended. Award marks for a well-supported opinion relevant to the issue. (2 marks)*

Should it be a crime to kill any wild animal? *(10 marks)*
1–14 (7 marks – 0.5 mark for each correct answer)
Sometimes alternatives are possible.

1. are	8. as
2. why	9. become
3. should	10. them
4. necessary, important, vital	11. that
5. If	12. other
6. and	13. is
7. second	14. best

15. *Open-ended. Award marks for an opinion relevant to the issue, supported by two appropriate reasons. (3 marks)*

Unit 22: Investigating English expressions

American English *(16 marks)*
1–16 (8 marks – 0.5 marks for each correct answer)

1. taxi	5. nappy	9. boot	13. tap
2. queue	6. handbag	10. petrol	14. pavement
3. autumn	7. sweets	11. dummy	15. curtains
4. lorry	8. trousers	12. sweet biscuits	16. lift

17 –24 (8 marks – 1 mark for each correct answer)

17. chemist	19. cooker	21. holiday	23. cinema/films
18. wardrobe	20. bonnet	22. rubbish	24. quid

Investigating idioms *(11 marks)*

1. white lie
2. Eyewash
3. A Tartar
4. A red herring
5. A blank cheque

6. a fool's paradise
7. a pig in a poke
8. Soft soap
9. A rough diamond
10. a square peg in a round hole

11. A fly in the ointment
12. a close shave
13. A mouthpiece
14. A hornets' nest

Word Classes Cup

UNIT 1 Word classes

We have reached the closing games in the Word Classes Cup! (A) and (B) are semi-finals. Count up the number of words for each team and put in the score. Count the same word more than once if it occurs more than once. For (C), put in the names of the winning teams from the semi-finals. Count the words and find out which team won. For "verbs", count only finite verbs, i.e. verbs which have a subject.

A. *Semi-final 1:* Nouns _____ v Pronouns _____
(Write the score.)

Last year, two teenage brothers in a small northern town tried to avoid their lessons. They pretended to be ill, so the school nurse rang their mum and she came to take them home. She looked after them well and asked a local doctor to come and give her advice. When the doctor arrived, he examined the boys but he was not completely sure what illness they had. He spoke to the mum and advised her to get or prepare a special kind of medicine.

B. *Semi-final 2:* Verbs _____ v Adverbs _____
(Write the score.)

After a few days, the mum overheard the two boys – Paul and Mike – when they were talking and laughing noisily with their friends, who often visited them at home. The boys claimed boastfully that they had successfully fooled the doctor and their mum. They stayed in bed lazily all day and happily watched films on television.

C. The final! _____ v _____
(Put in the names of the winning teams from (A) and (B). Then write the scores.)

Their mum was furious. The next morning, she pretended to be worried. She produced a bottle of medicine and made Paul swallow a spoonful. As soon as he had taken the "medicine", he jumped out of bed and rushed to the bathroom, where he was violently sick for more than ten minutes. Mike heard his brother being sick, so he slid out of bed, dressed and left the house as quickly as he could.
"I'm much better now," he told his mum. "Goodbye."
Ten minutes later, Paul staggered out of the bathroom, looking very weak and pale.
"I'm better too!" he told his mum. She smiled as she watched him go.

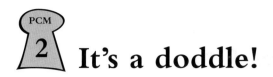

It's a doddle!

UNIT 2 Using standard English

- Match the slang or colloquial expression in (A) with the formal expression in (B).

A. Informal slang or colloquial expression	B. Formal, standard English expression
1. I'm **hard up** right now.	a) speechless; astonished
2. Don't get **taken in** by his story.	b) an informer
3. We were **put off** by the look of the food.	c) feeling very miserable
4. Watch out! The **fuzz** are coming.	d) short of money; penniless
5. We're **over the moon** with the result.	e) delighted; very pleased and excited
6. I was **struck dumb** when I heard about it.	f) spends a lot of time with; is friends with
7. His shoes are **really cool**.	g) deceived; tricked
8. Sunita was **down in the dumps**.	h) police
9. Tom **hangs around with** Mike and Jack.	i) very fashionable; attractive; impressive
10. People say he's a **snitch**.	j) deterred; made to dislike (something)

- Now try writing your own standard English versions of the informal expressions given.

A. Informal slang or colloquial expression	B. Formal, standard English expression
Somebody's **nicked** my pen!	
She was really **chuffed** with the present.	
Our new car is **a real winner**.	
What a **grotty-looking dump**!	
Don't be such a **sucker**.	
I can't go with you 'cuz **I'm skint**.	
Paul really **goofed** when he told you that.	
Phew! What is that **pong**?	
We had a **smashing** time at the party.	
The burglar **scarpered** before the police could **nab** him.	

Passive verbs

UNIT 3 Active and passive verbs 1

In a supermarket

Put in the passive Simple Present form of the verbs in brackets. Use **is** or **are + a past participle**, e.g. is sent, are given, is made, are sold.

British and American supermarkets are very similar in most ways, but American ones provide better facilities for customers. For example, when customers go to the check-out counter, their goods (1)_____ (pack) into bags for them, and their trolleys (2)_____ (push) out to their cars.

In most other ways, American and British supermarkets are similar. Popular items such as bread (3)_____ (put) at the far end of the store so that customers (4)_____ (force) to walk through the store to reach them. On their way, they (5)_____ (often attract) by goods which they did not intend to buy.

The layout of each store (6)_____ (design) to maximise sales. The store's own products (7)_____ (place) on shelves at waist height or slightly higher. Competing brands (8)_____ (keep) on lower or higher shelves. The colours of boxes (9)_____ (choose) to attract customers. Meanwhile soothing music (10) _____ (play) to keep customers happy while they fill their trolleys.

Getting new "parents"

Put in the passive Simple Past form of the verbs in brackets. Use **was** or **were + a past participle**, e.g. was eaten, were sent, was broken, were lost.

Even before the start of World War II in 1939, it was clear that the major cities in the United Kingdom would be bombed by German planes in the event of a war. Plans (1)_____ (prepare) to evacuate children to safer areas. When the war started, each child (2)_____ (give) a label and prepared for evacuation. Children (3)_____ (gather) in large groups. Then they (4)_____ (send) by rail to remote areas many miles away. People in rural areas (5)_____ (require) by law to take in one or more evacuees. Sometimes whole schools (6)_____ (evacuate) to a rural area. Classrooms in rural schools (7)_____ (share) with schools from unsafe city areas. The evacuees (8)_____ (welcome) by their new "parents". They (9)_____ (make) to feel like members of their new family and soon made friends. In this way, the lives of thousands of children (10) _____ (save).

Connectives crossword

Complete the crossword puzzle. All the words are connectives.

Across

1. We will serve refreshments _____ the performance.
5. _____ you are ready, give me a call.
6. They went bowling and out for dinner _____.
8. _____my maths homework, I have a book report to write.
12. Please sign the visitors' book _____ you leave.
13. I cannot fall asleep _____ I am tired.
14. We went outside _____ the cold weather.
16. _____ you hurry, you will be late.

Down

1. I said I would go, and _____ I will drive.
2. Do you prefer milk _____ juice?
3. I will wait _____ you get here before I leave.
4. I do not know _____ I will go now or later.
6. Holly _____ Molly went to the game.
7. I listened to music _____ I cleaned my room.
8. They will be late _____ they missed the bus.
9. _____ you finish soon, we can play.
10. We can leave immediately _____ your passport is valid.
11. I want to go to the cinema, _____ I don't have money for the ticket.
15. Don't go. She'll be here _____.

Sort them out!

UNIT 5 Forming complex sentences 1

- Match the **main clauses** with the correct **subordinate clauses**. On the line before each subordinate clause, write the number of the correct main clause.

main clauses	subordinate clauses
1. Butter will go soft	__ because of better health care.
2. Water will freeze in the garden	__ if you look directly at it.
3. Metal objects expand	__ after an earthquake below the seabed.
4. Earthquakes occur	__ if you leave it out of a fridge.
5. Indoor plants will die	__ when two underground "plates" collide.
6. A full moon is very bright	__ when there is a severe frost.
7. The sun can damage your eyes	__ before an earthquake under the sea.
8. A tsunami may occur	__ unless it is hidden by clouds.
9. Usually there is no warning	__ unless you water them regularly.
10. People are living longer	__ when you heat them.

- Now match the **subordinate clauses** with the correct **main clauses**. On the line after each subordinate clause, write the letter of the correct main clause.

subordinate clauses	main clauses
1. If you wash new jeans, __	a) shake the bottle.
2. Unless you clean your teeth, __	b) snails and frogs come out.
3. Before you pour out sauce, __	c) nobody seems to know.
4. Besides singing in a choir, __	d) ships had to carry more lifeboats.
5. When it rains, __	e) we both walked to school.
6. What his real job is __	f) we noticed the cracked windscreen.
7. After the "Titanic" sank, __	g) they may shrink.
8. Since the bus broke down, __	h) she played the piano.
9. As we were getting into our car, __	i) two ambulances raced by.
10. While we were waiting for a bus, __	j) you may have painful toothache.

PCM 6 Punctuation posers

UNIT 6 Punctuation

Match them up

There is one punctuation mark missing from each sentence. Draw a line from the sentence to the punctuation mark that is missing. Then mark the place in the sentence where the punctuation mark should go. Use each punctuation mark once only.

. full stop	
, comma	
' apostrophe	
; semi colon	
: colon	

1. "Ah That's the type of bike I'd like one day!"
2. We gave Grandma her favourite present a box of chocolates.
3. Although the Browns are on holiday, theres a light on in their house.
4. "We can get to the park through here, can't we" they asked.
5. Sarah discovered the culprit a cheeky little mouse in the cupboard.
6. Susan showed various symptoms a fever, nausea and general weakness.
7. "What time does the show start Mike?"
8. Mary splurged on new shoes Matthew thought she was extravagant.
9. "I can't find my watch, Paul said. "Have you seen it?"
10. Turn the light off you're wasting electricity.

! exclamation mark	
? question mark	
" speech mark	
— dash	
( ) brackets	

Oliver Twist

Find and correct 14 punctuation mistakes in the following passage. Underline and then correct each mistake. You may need to change, add or omit punctuation marks and capital letters.

When Oliver Twist was nine he lived in a workhouse one day he was so hungry that he asked for more soup and was promptly seized by the master.

The village elders were holding a serious meeting when Mr Bumble the beadle or village policeman rushed into the room in great excitement he addressed the gentleman in the high chair and said "Mr Limbkins I beg your pardon, sir! Oliver Twist has asked for more!"

A look of horror appeared on every face.

"For more" exclaimed Mr Limbkins. Control yourself, Bumble and answer me clearly. Do I understand that he asked for more, after he had eaten the normal supper"

"He did, sir," replied Bumble still in a state of shock.

"That boy will be hanged," said Mr Limbkins "I know that boy will be hanged."

(adapted from Oliver Twist *by Charles Dickens)*

Recount of an earthquake

UNIT 8 Active and passive verbs 2

- Find and underline ten passive verbs in the following passage. It is an English translation of an account by an Indonesian girl on the island of Nias, off the Sumatran coast. She is telling a reporter what happened to her when there was a severe earthquake under the sea in March 2005.

At about 11.15 p.m. I was asleep in my home near Gunung Sitoli. Then something woke me up and I felt the ground trembling and shaking. Our house was rocked from side to side. I was sure that it was going to fall down. I was right because the roof started to collapse. I was thrown to the ground by the force of the earthquake. When the roof and walls fell in, I was buried under piles of corrugated iron and wood. My right leg was trapped by heavy pieces of timber and concrete. I called to my parents in the next room but there was no reply. Later on, I was told that they were killed when the roof collapsed on them.

I called out for a long time, but nobody came. Then it started to rain and the water came in on me. After some time, I heard somebody shouting in the road outside, so I called out as loudly as I could. Luckily for me, my shouts were heard by a neighbour. Somebody called to me and I answered. Men started to dig and at last I was rescued. I was lifted out of the wreckage and somebody put me on a stretcher. Then I was brought here to the hospital because of my injuries.

- Choose five of the passive verbs from the passage above. Use them in your own sentences. Do not copy from the passage.

_____

_____

_____

_____

_____

What does it mean?

UNIT 9 Official language

Read each passage of official language. Underline the words in the passage with the same meaning as the words given below it.

A.

> I am directed by the Chief Executive to acknowledge receipt of your letter of the tenth instant (with enclosures) and to say that the suggestions contained therein have been referred to the Accounts Department for further consideration and report. A further communication will be sent to you when the outcome of the above-mentioned study is to hand.

1. told, ordered
2. thank you for
3. of this month
4. in it
5. sent
6. letter
7. result
8. available

B.

> In response to your interesting enquiry, I am happy to confirm that the referee's decision mentioned in your email was correct. In my opinion, it certainly does not warrant the remedial action urged by you.
>
> The offside rule is quite clear but not universally understood. A player is deemed to be *onside* if, at the moment when a ball is kicked to or past him, there is at least one member of the opposing team (excluding the goalkeeper) nearer to the opposing goal-line than he is himself. A significant point here, and one which is frequently overlooked by uninformed spectators and commentators, is that the question whether or not a player is offside is determined by where he is standing at the moment when a ball is kicked towards an opponent's goal and NOT where he is when a ball reaches him from behind.

1. reply
2. justify
3. setting right
4. put forward strongly
5. widely; by everybody
6. judged, considered
7. not counting, leaving out
8. very important, crucial
9. ignored, forgotten
10. decided

Investigating clauses

UNIT 10 Forming complex sentences 2

- On the line after each sentence write the **number of words** in the **main clause**. Use each of the numbers 1–10 **once only**.

1. Stop where Mary is waiting for us. ____
2. Although Mr Wright no longer collects stamps, he still has thousands of stamps stored in his home. ____
3. Where have you put the books that Mum bought for us? ____
4. When an earthquake affected the island of Nias, hundreds of people were killed or seriously injured. ____
5. Paul will tell us when we can start. ____
6. The car which had been following us disappeared. ____
7. Some of the players who once won the World (Soccer) Cup for England are no longer alive now. ____
8. Stand up if you know the answer. ____
9. The district where we live is very peaceful. ____
10. The old man who is talking to Anne is her friend's grandfather. ____

- Look at the ten subordinate clauses in sentences 1–10 above. Write the number of each sentence below to show the type of subordinate clause in it. You should find five adjectival clauses, four adverbial clauses and one noun clause.

adjectival: _____

adverbial: _____

noun: _____

- Write three sentences of your own, each one with a different type of subordinate clause.

1. (adjectival) _____

_____

2. (adverbial) _____

_____

3. (noun) _____

_____

Call the Coastguard!

Unit 11 Making notes

1. You are Kate Ellis. Your mother and brother are out. Your father is fishing from a motorboat at sea. You received the following phone call on your mobile phone at 4.05 p.m. from your father. Make notes to tell both the Coastguard and your mother.

"Hello, is that you, Katie? Oh! Good! Is Mum there? Oh! I see. Well, you'll have to save us. Have you got a pencil? Right. We went fishing in John Burton's motorboat – the three of us: me, John and John's brother. Now we're about a mile east of Bishop's Rock. Phone the Coastguard urgently, please. Tell them that our engine has packed up. We're drifting eastwards with the current. It will be dark in a couple of hours and I'm worried that we'll drift into the path of a ship. We don't have any flares or rockets. Have you got that? A mile east of Bishop's Rock. Three men in a motorboat. When you've got through to the coastguard, please ring me back. You've got my number, but it's 047-0633. And please tell Mum when she comes in. That's all. Love to everybody."

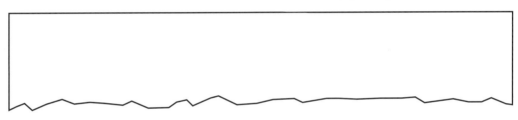

2. Here is what the Coastguard Officer told you. Make notes so that you can phone your father back (and tell your mother) what's happening.

"What's his mobile phone number, please? We'll try to contact him ourselves directly. If you speak to him as well, tell him we'll send a rescue helicopter to locate the boat and a rescue craft to tow the boat back into harbour. If they've got any torches or flares, tell them to use them to help us locate them more quickly. Hopefully, we should find them within the next hour."

3. Katie's father phoned her back an hour later. These are the notes she took during that call. Can you reconstruct his message in full sentences?

5.15 p.m. D phnd. Found by Cgd resc cft. Heli missing!!! D + mates cold, wet – OK. Shd be back harbr by bish. Will phn agn then. Don't wait dinner.

The Wickham Rainbow

UNIT 12 Writing a summary

- The news reports below follow the same story. Read the reports and then complete the activity at the bottom of the page.

2nd May The "Wickham Rainbow", pride of the Greenstar Line was launched at Belfast and fitted out for her first Mediterranean cruise. The "Wickham" was the largest liner afloat and was capable of carrying over 3000 passengers and crew. The vessel cost over £450 million and was insured for £500 million.

6th June The "Wickham" set off on its maiden voyage, bound for Spain, Italy, Cyprus, Greek Islands, Malta and Tunisia. Carrying 2420 passengers, the liner called at Lisbon, Gibraltar and Naples. Shortly after passing through the Strait of Messina, the ship reported a major explosion in the area of its bow. The ship sank within 20 minutes. 1864 people were rescued but over 1000 passengers and crew perished, making the disaster the worst in recent history. Terrorist activity was suspected but no proof was obtained. The British government promised a full enquiry.

12th July Divers have completed their investigation of the wreck of the "Wickham", now lying in water 120 metres deep off the southern tip of Italy. All the evidence points to a World War II mine which hit the bow of the liner and exploded on impact, producing a hole through which a torrent of water poured, flooding and sinking the ship within 20 minutes. Over the last fifty years, four other old mines have been detected and rendered safe around the southern coast of Italy. Divers report that some of the ship's lifeboats had not been launched because of the steep angle at which the liner sank. It is understood that underwriters have agreed to pay the Greenstar Line the full sum insured of £500 million, and that the payment will have an adverse effect on major insurance companies in Britain, America and Germany.

- Today is the 14th of July. The report of the divers has just been issued. What headlines might we expect to see in the following three newspapers? All three newspapers took into account the events of May and June when reporting the discoveries made by the divers.

a) The *Daily Wag* favours sensational reporting, highlighting individuals and human interest.

b) The *Weekly Moneybag* is concerned almost entirely with business, money and events that affect profits.

c) The *Daily Facts* tries to present an unsensational account of the main facts.

Editing

PCM 12

UNIT 13 Editing

Edit these two passages written by pupils about their hobby. Correct ten obvious mistakes in each of them. Then make any other editorial changes that you think will improve the writing.

Fishing

My hobby is fishing. Whenever I get a opportunity, I go to the Seven Islands pond on Mitcham Common with my friends. We cannot affort to buy fishing-rods, so we catch our fish by dragging. I will explane how we do it.

First, we find an old sack what nobody wants. We slit one side of the sack and open it out so that it is like a large net. Then we waid into the pool in pairs, each of us holds one side of the sack. We drag the sack threw the water for a few yards. Then we pull it up and look to see what we have caught, if anything.

On one occasion, we caught a jack, a young pike. It was too long to put in my small jar, so I searched amongst the bushes untill I found a large milk-bottle. I stuck the jack in the bottle head first and hurried home on a bus. Then I released the fish into a big pond in a nursry behind my house. The friendly owner always lets me put fish in his pond, so there was plenty of small fish for the jack to chase.

Cooking

When I have some liesure time at home, I like to cook, that is very conveniant for my family because my father and brother like to eat anything I cook. In fact, I'm very poplar at home and with my neighbours.

My mother is a very experienced and skillful cook, so I have learned a lot by helping her. I often watch cookery programms on television and print recipes from the computer, when one of my neighbour has a birthday, I usually cook a special cake as a present.

When I was younger, I only cooked British dishes but now I am learning French and Italian cooking beside. Continental cooking is more complicated then English cooking and involves using more spices and ingrediants to give the food better flavour.

What if?

UNIT 14 Conditional sentences

What if things aren't as we know they are or if things hadn't happened in the way we know they happened? Can you think of possible alternative consequences? For example:

| If Christopher Columbus hadn't discovered America | then | we would have far fewer programmes on our TV! |

- Complete these "what ifs" with your own ideas.

| If dinosaurs hadn't become extinct | then | |

| If the Earth were square and not round | then | |

| If the telephone had not yet been invented | then | |

| If people and animals could speak the same language | then | |

| If Arthur had not pulled the sword from the stone | then | |

- Now make up your own complete "what ifs".

| If | then | |

| If | then | |

PCM 14 The war against the moles

UNIT 16 Narrative writing

Read this extract from *Growing Up With Sally* by Anne Milbray. Then answer the questions about it.

Sally arrived at her uncle's house just in time to hear the solemn declaration of war.

"I'm fed up with those blinking moles!" her uncle moaned. "Just look at our lawn! I hereby declare war on all moles! Maybe you can give me a hand."

Sally's loyalties were divided: she loved animals, but she sympathised with Uncle John. His lawn was littered with unsightly molehills.

"I've bought some traps," Uncle John confided in a half-whisper, "but don't tell your aunt. She wouldn't even kill a spider, let alone a mole. I don't want to upset her."

The next day, Sally's aunt went shopping. As soon as she had gone, Uncle John dug into the molehills and set traps with great relish. He dropped mothballs down two holes and stuck a hosepipe down another one. Not wanting to miss out on any method, he took a spade and dug under two molehills. Sally watched and helped when she could. She admired her uncle's determination, but was secretly relieved when all his efforts proved to be in vain. The moles pushed out the traps and ignored mothballs, floods and spades. Safe below the ground, they stuck their tongues out at their enemies.

Uncle John retreated to his desk to lick his wounds and search through his gardening magazines. "I suppose I could fit a pipe to the exhaust on the car and try to gas them," he told Sally, "but there are too many holes. The fumes would disperse too quickly."

A week later, the postman brought an unexpected end to the war. He delivered a small box to Uncle John. Sally watched him open it and take out some small bulbs. "They're called Sork," he explained. "They come from Sweden. You drop them down the mole holes and they give off an odour that moles detest. Well, that's what the advertisement claims. Let's give them a try."

Sally was sceptical – but what do you know? Six months later, Sally returned to her uncle's and – guess what – no mole-hills! The lawn was free for games again. Apparently, the moles had emigrated to sweeter-smelling pastures.

Final score: Uncle 1 – Moles 0.

1. Find at least three places where time connectives are used to mark the passage of time.
2. Why does "uncle" sometimes start with a small letter and sometimes with a capital letter?
3. In what way do lines 1 and 2 show a contrast?
4. Why does Uncle John use "hereby" in line 2?
5. In line 4, which words after the colon give information about a word before the colon?
6. What figure of speech is "to lick his wounds" and what does it mean in the extract?
7. How would you describe the tone of the author? What evidence do you have to support your view?
8. What do you suppose Sally thought of the result of the "war"? What is your reason for your answer?

School report

Imagine you were allowed to write your own school report. What would you say about yourself? Use the frame below to write a report for this term. Remember to use:

- verbs in the present tense;
- impersonal style;
- descriptive adjectives and adverbs;
- precise language such as facts and figures.

SCHOOL REPORT		
NAME:	CLASS:	DATE:
ENGLISH		
MATHS		
SCIENCE		
HISTORY		
GEOGRAPHY		
MUSIC		
ART		
PHYSICAL EDUCATION		
SUMMARY		

Cockney rhyming slang

UNIT 22 Investigating English expressions

"Cockney" is the term used to describe a person born within the sound of the bells of St Mary-Le-Bow Church in Cheapside, London. Cockney rhyming slang is a code where standard English words can be replaced by the abbreviated forms of well-known phrases rhyming with them.

Standard word	Cockney rhyming slang	Sentence
believe	Adam and Eve	I don't Adam and Eve it!

- Can you match the standard word with the Cockney rhyming slang?

Standard word	Cockney rhyming slang
stairs	bacon and eggs
money	trouble and strife
time	brown bread
wife	dog and bone
road	whistle and flute
suit	apples and pears
mouth	jam tart
phone	bees and honey
shoes	frog and toad
legs	lager and lime
dead	north and south
heart	ones and twos

- Find the Cockney rhyming slang for some more words.

Standard word	Cockney rhyming slang

mind your loaf of bread

- Try writing some dialogue between two Cockney characters.

Notes